Peace Meets the Streets

Peace Meets the Streets

On the Ground in
Northern Ireland, 1993–2001

James M. Lyons

PEACE MEETS THE STREETS
ON THE GROUND IN NORTHERN IRELAND, 1993–2001

iUniverse books may be ordered through booksellers or by contacting:

iUniverse LLC
1663 Liberty Drive
Bloomington, IN 47403
www.iuniverse.com
1-800-Authors (1-800-288-4677)

ISBN: 978-1-4917-3769-9 (sc)
ISBN: 978-1-4917-3768-2 (e)

Library of Congress Control Number: 2014914477

Printed in the United States of America.

iUniverse rev. date: 09/24/2014

For Marcia

Sine Qua Nihil

Contents

Preface

This book chronicles some of the highlights of my eight years of public service in Northern Ireland, 1993–2001. During that time, I made innumerable trips to and from Ireland. (I stopped counting at fifty—trips on Air Force One not included). Generally, I traveled alone, but from time to time Marcia or one of the kids would join me. These trips were always special for me.

These years were among the most challenging and satisfying of my professional life. It is my hope to share with my family and friends some of the challenges, excitement, frustrations, and achievements of this extraordinary time in the long continuum of Irish history. Also, those who study or follow Irish affairs and history might find this chapter to be of interest.

This book is built around some remarkable men and women who struggled each day to improve their society and their future: a solitary Catholic woman in far West Belfast who searched for over twenty years for the remains of her "disappeared" son; one of Ulster's leading Anglo-Irish figures, a businessman who fought for social justice at risk to his life; an ex-convict turned politician and peace figure; longtime community workers on the ground in West, North, and East Belfast; and tireless community leaders from both communities in Derry. Their stories shape my story and ultimately those critical years in Northern Ireland, 1993–2001.

The story requires some political context; after all, Northern Ireland is itself an artificial political entity created by partition to end the Irish War of Independence in 1921. Indispensable political roles were played by President Bill Clinton and First Lady Hillary Clinton, Senator George

Mitchell, British Prime Ministers John Major and Tony Blair, and Irish Prime Ministers Reynolds, Bruton, and Ahern. Mo Mowlam, secretary of state for Northern Ireland, and Dermot Gallagher, Irish ambassador to the United States, were key to the peace process, and both became my trusted friends. The International Fund for Ireland (IFI), its staff and board, and its indefatigable chairman, Willie McCarter, were the vehicle through which reconciliation and prosperity were supported by the United States, the European Union, Canada, New Zealand, and Australia. The IFI's role in this story is central.

But, in the end, the story is of remarkable people on the ground, from Belfast to Fahan, Dundalk to Derry, Coalisland to Enniskillen, Omagh to Armagh, and all points in between. Their persistent will, leadership, and courage made peace meet the streets.

A Brief History of Northern Ireland

A bit of history of Northern Ireland by way of orientation is in order.

Ireland—before partition in 1921—consisted of thirty-two counties and was part of the United Kingdom of England, Scotland, and Wales. The history of English rule dated from the Normans in the eleventh and twelfth centuries. In the early years, English dominance had been largely confined to the Dublin area ("The Pale") beyond which the Irish tribes held sway. Viking invasions (and interbreeding and marriage) had produced a race of fierce Irish Celts who gave their allegiance to tribal chieftains.

Repeated efforts to subjugate the tribes by the Norman/English were finally completed with the defeat of the remaining chieftains in Donegal in 1607. The two last Irish chieftains—"the Earls"—left for Spain and France in the "Flight of the Earls," and English rule was solidified in the north.

To populate the vacated earldoms with loyal subjects, the British crown brought Protestant immigrants from Scotland and England in a program known as "the Ulster Plantation." Tensions between these new "Scots Irish" or "Anglo-Irish" and the indigenous Irish was immediate, as the Scots and Anglo-Irish gentry exercised minority rule with little or no regard for the largely peasant majority (Catholic) population.

After centuries of strife, the culmination came in the Battle of the Boyne, in which the English throne hung in the balance. The forces of Protestant William of Orange met those of his Catholic son-in-law, James, and decisively defeated the Jacobites in July 1690, in a running battle along the Boyne river valley. The "Orange Order"—reflecting William's Dutch House of Orange—was created to commemorate this sectarian victory;

annual parades are still held throughout Northern Ireland during July. It is a continuing source of friction and often violence between the two communities.

Over the next two centuries, repeated efforts at Irish independence were made. One of the most prominent was led by Wolfe Tone in 1798 with assistance from Napoleon ("the Year of the French"); it failed, the French withdrew, and Tone and his Fenian leaders were hanged in Dublin.

A later rising was led by Irish legend, nationalist, and orator Robert Emmet; he, too, failed and was hanged in Kilmainham Gaol in Dublin in 1803. A few decades later, Charles Stewart Parnell, a popular and charismatic Irish politician, campaigned for home rule. After a notorious affair with the married Kitty O'Shea, he was driven from power and died prematurely in disgrace at age forty-five in 1891.

Of note and common to Tone, Emmet, and Parnell is that each of them, ardent Irish nationalists, was a Protestant, not a Catholic.

In 1916, a group of Irish revolutionaries staged a planned rising during Easter week of that year. Led by Patrick Pearse and James Connolly, the armed but tiny "citizen's army" hoped to take advantage of the British preoccupation with World War I to secure Irish independence. This was despite the fact that a significant majority of Irish favored continued union with Great Britain. After several days of attacks and counterattacks in central Dublin, the British military put down the Easter Rising with brutal force, declared martial law, and executed the leaders by firing squad at Kilmainham. One leader, Joseph Mary Plunkett, severely wounded in the Rising, was brought from his hospital bed and strapped to a chair in the Kilmainham yard so he could be shot.

Spared execution but sentenced to prison were Eamon de Valera, a dual citizen of the United States and Ireland whose execution it was thought would be poorly received in the United States, and Countess Constance Gore-Booth Markievicz, who was second in command of Irish forces at St. Stephens Green during the Rising. Although Markievicz, an Irish-born revolutionary who had married a Polish count, herself objected, the British decided not to execute her because she was female. After she was released from prison, she was the first woman elected to the British Parliament, but, as a member of Sinn Fein, she declined to take the oath of allegiance to the King and did not take her seat.

The Irish population was outraged at martial law and the executions. Public support grew for home rule and independence. The Irish revolutionaries—now the Irish Republican Army led by Michael Collins—waged a guerilla war for independence. In 1921, after years of terrorism on both sides and fueled by the brutal tactics of British paramilitaries known as the "Black and Tans," a treaty was signed granting twenty-six counties of Ireland "home rule" within the Commonwealth and creating the new province of Northern Ireland, consisting of six counties from the Ulster region. Thus, out of centuries of tension, war, terror, and sectarianism, Northern Ireland was born as a province of the United Kingdom.

However, this did not end the violence on the island. Those nationalists outraged at the treaty and the partition took to arms, and Ireland in the south fell into civil war. Terror and violence once again erupted between those who supported the treaty of home rule and those who saw it as a sellout. After the assassination of IRA Commandant Michael Collins in County Cork, a reconciliation of a sort was achieved and the Irish Free State declared. After World War II—in which the Free State was neutral—Ireland became a full and independent republic in 1947.

In Northern Ireland, partition and the treaty brought no end to the violence. The IRA, determined to reunite Northern Ireland and the Republic of Ireland, continued its guerilla and terrorist attacks. These were countered by harsh retaliation from Loyalist paramilitary groups such as the Ulster Volunteer Force (UVF) and Ulster Defense Association (UDA) and police suppression from the RUC (Royal Ulster Constabulary). They were assisted by the British Army and its elite paratrooper unit, the SAS.

Political gerrymandering was used to limit or, in some cases, eliminate Catholic/nationalist political representation with the result that unionists/loyalists dominated many if not most local district councils and the local parliament at Stormont in Belfast.

Patterns of anti-Catholic discrimination infected housing, employment, and educational systems and severely diminished opportunities for the Catholic population. Nobel Peace Prize laureate David Trimble, the leading Unionist politician, later described Northern Ireland during this period as "a cold house for Catholics."

Nevertheless, Northern Ireland was relatively peaceful in the 1950s and 1960s during the postwar period of general economic prosperity in the UK and Europe. However, the decline of the two major industries in Northern Ireland, ship building and textiles, led to a deteriorating economic outlook, competition for fewer jobs, and increasing tensions between both communities. Civil rights movements in the Catholic community, patterned on the civil rights movement in the United States and the "Prague Spring," took root, while sectarian violence escalated, most notably in Derry in the so-called Battle of the Bogside in 1969. Shortly thereafter, the British Army was deployed by London to maintain order.

At first welcomed as protectors by the nationalist community, the British Army soon came to be regarded as tools of British repression like the RUC. Even modest political and social reform efforts failed in the face of hard-line Loyalist opposition, personified by the inflammatory Ian Paisley and his Democratic Ulster Party (DUP), whose slogan for reform was "never, never, never." The IRA was declared illegal, and a policy of internment without public trial for suspected terrorists and sympathizers was begun. Moderate Catholic legislative members withdrew from Stormont and cancelled support for local government.

In January 1972, British paratroopers, claiming to have been fired upon, opened fire on a large, unarmed Catholic crowd engaged in a Sunday civil rights march in Derry's Bogside. Fourteen unarmed civilians were killed and scores of others wounded in the event that became known as "Bloody Sunday." The Catholic population throughout Northern Ireland and the Republic of Ireland was enraged, and new recruits flocked to the Provisional IRA ("the Provos"), which had broken with the increasingly Maoist "traditional" IRA. In March of that year, the British Parliament dissolved the local parliament at Stormont and instituted direct rule of

Northern Ireland from London. The era of the modern "Troubles" was born.

For the next thirty years, despite various efforts at peace and proportional government like the Sunningdale Agreement, sectarian violence cursed the province. Over three thousand men, women, and children were killed or injured during this period, often at random or as a result of a targeted terrorist bomb. An already deteriorating private economy worsened, while security forces increased and repair (e.g., glass) and construction industries were in demand. Derry and Belfast were especially hard hit: virtually every building in the center of the old walled city of Derry was destroyed or damaged, and Belfast became synonymous with Beirut.

In 1985, new government leaders, Prime Minister John Major of Great Britain and *Taoiseach* (Prime Minister) Albert Reynolds of the Republic of Ireland, reached an agreement of joint cooperation for Northern Ireland. Known as the Anglo-Irish Agreement, it was a recognition of the interests of both governments in a cooperative resolution of the violence and social disorder. (More about the Agreement comes later.) Campaigns of violence on both sides continued; however, the Agreement held, and an uneasy stalemate took hold. While acts of terrorism decreased somewhat, the atmosphere in the province was still volatile, precarious, and dangerous.

Across the Atlantic in the United States, change had also come to the executive branch of the federal government. After twelve years of Republican occupancy of the White House and little, if any, interest in Northern Ireland, Governor Bill Clinton of Arkansas, a Democrat, was elected and took office in January 1993.

My part of the story of Northern Ireland begins there.

Chapter One

Dundalk

Dundalk lies in County Louth in the Republic of Ireland, on the border with Northern Ireland and astride the main road from Dublin to Belfast. Dating from Celtic times, the town was invaded and taken by the Normans, who fortified it and made it the northern limit of the Pale, the area held by the Normans around Dublin. ("Beyond the Pale" comes from these lands not subject to English law or control.)

In the seventeenth century, Lord Limerick laid out the town around the still quaint market square. During the Troubles it was reputed to be a frequent border refuge for IRA operatives and earned the nicknames "El Paso" and "Gun-dalk." It is a charming market town of some twenty thousand souls that on a cold and windy night in December 2000 swelled to over fifty thousand in the market square. They were there to see and hear Bill Clinton on his third and farewell tour to Ireland as a sitting President of the United States.

The President was, of course, running late, in part due to weather and in part due to his habitual tardiness. (He just can't ever bring himself to say good-bye and move on according to schedule.) But this made little or no matter to the people who had begun to gather as early as midafternoon to hear his evening speech. A great platform had been erected in the town square and was surrounded by Irish and American flags and banners awash in bright lights. Bands took turns entertaining the crowd with traditional and popular music. A huge American flag had been hung on the Georgian-style bank across the square. Rain was in the cool air but never arrived. A cloudy and dark night provided a dramatic backdrop for a growing mood of an electric evening. And it was every bit of that.

The presidential delegation included dignitaries like my good friends from Wyoming, former governor and now US Ambassador Mike Sullivan and his wife, Jane; Baltimore Mayor Martin O'Malley; Senators Chris Dodd and Patrick Leahy; and a host of Irish American congressmen and congresswomen. We had bussed to Dundalk from earlier events in Dublin. While waiting in the ornate brass and marble lobby of the local bank opened to us for the evening, we talked among ourselves of the history of which we were a part. At one point I went out to visit with excited young people at the rope line. Mostly, we waited for the President and watched the excitement build. But, for me, it was a time of reflection amidst the noise and exciting atmosphere.

Seven years earlier, in November 1993, I had first arrived as the new, presidentially appointed US observer to the International Fund for Ireland. In recent years, I had taken on additional duties, succeeding Senator George Mitchell as Special Advisor to the President and Secretary of State for economic initiatives in Northern Ireland and the border counties of the Republic of Ireland. I had been to Ireland and back, north and south, more than fifty times, and this was my third trip with the President. During those seven years, I had spent part of every day on Irish affairs, whether in Denver, the State Department, the White House, or on the ground in Ireland. I had made lasting friends and had had rare and exhilarating experiences. Now it was coming to an official end. And that night in Dundalk, I was transported back in my mind to how it all began.

Chapter Two

Beginnings

In the mid-seventies, I worked as a young partner and trial lawyer in Denver, striving to learn and improve my craft. A series of antitrust cases against the companies of the Bell system took me around the country, doing discovery—the often tedious but necessary process of reviewing documents, interviewing and preparing witnesses, and getting a massive case ready for trial. One of the cases was in Arkansas against Southwestern Bell.

Knowing I was being sent to Little Rock to conduct the initial discovery, my friend and fellow Denver lawyer Mike Driver suggested that I look up one Bill Clinton in Little Rock. Mike described him as our age (twenty-eight) and a lawyer "with the Attorney General's Office." Mike knew Clinton from back east and the student moratorium against the Vietnam War in 1968, and he thought we might enjoy meeting. So, finishing my work early and with time to kill, I called Bill Clinton. He invited me to drop by the Attorney General's Office to say hello and for a cup of coffee.

Over coffee, we talked about Driver, Denver, and our backgrounds. The conversation then turned to the case that brought me to Little Rock. The North American Telecommunications Association (NATA) had been formed in Washington, DC, to represent its member companies, who manufactured or sold customer premises equipment in competition with the Bell system companies. The association and its anti-Bell strategy was the brainchild of a brilliant lawyer named Ed Spievack, who had retained me to work with him on national regulatory and litigation matters. One of NATA's members, Fisk Telephone Company, was trying to do business in Arkansas and was feeling the full weight of Bell's predatory practices.

As Clinton listened, he showed increasing interest, particularly as the effects of predatory pricing for competitive products and services by the Bell system would come at the expense of Arkansas consumers. Representing the agency charged with consumer protection, he wondered what the Attorney General's Office might do. Sensing an opportunity, I suggested they might consider intervening in our case and asked Clinton to introduce me to the attorney general. He replied, "I *am* the attorney general." When I expressed disbelief and looked flabbergasted, he took me to the glass doors of the office through which I had entered. There, underneath the seal of the state of Arkansas, read "Bill Clinton, Attorney General." It was a rather awkward but humorous start to what became an enduring friendship.

The Attorney General's Office did intervene, with mixed results. While we did not get all the relief we had sought, we did get some rate relief in Arkansas and valuable discovery and insight into the pricing and cost-shifting practices of the Bell system. This we would later find useful in federal antitrust cases *Jarvis, et al. v. AT&T, et al.* and *Selectron v. AT&T, et al.* These cases were precursors to the case filed by the US Justice Department that led to the breakup of the Bell system in 1986, and our cases were settled on very favorable terms for the industry we represented.

I continued developing a career in banking and trial work while becoming more involved in local and national politics. Over the years, this interest kept me in contact with Governor Clinton and his remarkable wife, attorney Hillary Clinton. I was on his prodigious Rolodex, a list later known as the "FOBs," Friends of Bill. I became friends with his most trusted and key advisor, Little Rock attorney Bruce Lindsey, and his intense chief of staff, Betsey Wright. We maintained regular contact, and I helped him with gubernatorial and Democratic national campaigns, fundraising in Denver and Aspen while expanding his Rocky Mountain contacts. He served five terms as governor and gained a rising national reputation throughout the 1980s. He was clearly on the move beyond Arkansas.

In 1987, Senator Gary Hart of Colorado again sought the Democratic nomination for president. He had narrowly lost the nomination to Vice President Walter Mondale in 1984 and was back stronger than ever. Although I wasn't directly involved in his campaign, I became caught up in the excitement his bid brought to Denver. I, too, felt the painful disappointment when he abruptly left the race in the Donna Rice scandal. A few days later, Betsey Wright called. Would I come to Little Rock for a weekend to discuss the 1988 presidential race with a few of his friends from around the country? I agreed and flew to Arkansas. There, for the first time, I met and was introduced to the Clintons' inner circle of remarkable people, including Mickey Kantor, Sandy Berger, Harold Ickes, Webb Hubbell, and Vince Foster. I also renewed ties with an old Chicago political acquaintance, lawyer and high school friend of Hillary, Kevin O'Keefe. We quickly rebonded and went on to become fast friends.

Organized by Hillary Clinton and Betsey Wright, the weekend conference debated the pros, cons, and prospects of a presidential race by a forty-year-old moderate Democrat southern governor in the aftermath of Jimmy Carter. The press dogged our every move, including a furtive jog he and I took by going over the back fence of the governor's mansion without security. In the end, after tantalizing the press, Bill decided the time was not right. As we decompressed over a Sunday dinner at the Capitol Hotel, however, each of us knew the day would come. And, in 1991, it arrived.

In the spring of 1991, President George H. W. Bush (number forty-one) enjoyed unprecedented approval ratings from the Gulf War. None of the so-called major Democrat possibilities, including Governor Mario Cuomo of New York and Senator Bill Bradley of New Jersey, stepped forward to challenge the then-popular president, and he looked secure for a second term. But Bill Clinton, schooled in years of study and travel around the country as the head of the Democratic Leadership Council (DLC), thought Bush could be beaten. As a keynote speaker for the DLC convention in Cleveland that May, Clinton showed his remarkable charisma and brought down the house. Vigorously highlighting themes of reduced government spending, welfare reform, and personal responsibility, he called for a new Democratic covenant. And thus was born the Clinton presidential campaign of 1992.

In September, a core group gathered in Washington to organize the campaign. Mickey Kantor, a longtime Clinton friend and Democratic activist from California, chaired the meeting and delivered our assignments. I was assigned responsibility of chairing a group of lawyers from around the country to provide legal advice and structure to the campaign. This ad hoc group included longtime Clinton friends like Vince Foster, Bruce Lindsey, Alston Johnson in Baton Rouge, and Jim Hamilton in Washington, DC. We formed state campaign committees and researched state election laws, ballot access questions, and primary rules in each of our respective regions. Also included were more ordinary tasks such as contracts and campaign office leases, employment questions, and financial commitments. I also undertook an effort to set up master banking relationships for early campaign funds against which the campaign borrowed until federal matching funds became available as we qualified for them in state after state.

Told and retold, the story of the Clinton campaign 1991–1992 has taken on an aura of both myth and history. Documentaries like *The War Room* caught some of the frantic nature of the campaign. John Travolta and Emma Thompson made a clumsy and fictional stab at portraying the Clintons in *Primary Colors*, based on the Joel Klein novel. Some accounts are partially accurate and others wildly exaggerated, but all are interesting or amusing to me. I do not propose to retell my version here—confidentiality is still the hallmark of lawyering. But needless to say, we went from "Bill who, from Hope where" to President of the United States in seventeen tumultuous months. And it was simply exhilarating.

On the morning after the election, I received an early call at the Capitol Hotel in Little Rock. Trying to get some sleep after an exhausting twenty-four-hour, cross-country election marathon whose last stop had been Denver, I awoke to an immediate request. Would I please come to the governor's mansion right away? The governor, now president-elect, wanted to see me and Kevin O'Keefe, organizer and the mastermind who managed Illinois for Clinton/Gore, which had cinched the nomination in March. After passing through the now omnipresent Secret Service, we met him in the kitchen, getting coffee. It was the first time I addressed him as "Mr. President" (and the only way I have addressed him since). After the hugs and congratulations, Clinton asked us what we wanted to do in

Washington. He assumed we wanted to join him. Neither Kevin nor I had given any previous thought to this question. We both demurred and promised to get back to him soon. In the meantime, I stayed in Little Rock and was appointed to the transition team as Counsel to the Office of the President-Elect. Dividing my time between Little Rock, Washington, and Denver, I enjoyed my temporary role and being intimately involved with the upcoming transition of power. We had roughly seventy days to form the first Democratic administration since Jimmy Carter. We were inundated with position papers, resumes, and advice—solicited and unsolicited. All of it needed to be reviewed, sifted, and put into a manageable form for the president-elect to consider while keeping in mind that we were now making a historical record to be preserved by law in the Archives of the United States.

Inauguration Day, January 20, 1993, a cold but sunny day, marked a special time for my family and me. Together with the O'Keefes, Marcia and I sat in the VIP grandstand on the west steps of the US Capitol and watched from a mere thirty feet away as Al Gore and then our friend took the oaths of office. We looked out over the more than 250,000 Americans gathered on the capitol grounds for this uniquely American and historic event. Later, my entire family enjoyed cookies and hot chocolate while watching the parade from the comfort of the presidential box on Pennsylvania Avenue. A round of Inaugural Balls capped the extraordinary day.

Flying home to Denver after the festivities, I felt satisfied with a job well done. I also thought my days in Washington would be occasional and pleasantly social. Determined to maintain our friendship, I planned to support the President in any possible way. I did not, however, expect or want anything or a job in the administration. Nor did I intend to lobby the Clinton White House. All I intended to do was be a friend to the Clintons—both during and after his presidency.

Chapter Three

The Irish Observer

In early 1993, the White House asked me to consider senior legal positions in several major agencies of the federal government. I declined, just as I had already declined a federal judgeship offered to me during the transition. My lack of Washington experience, my family from whom I had been away for long stretches during the campaign, and my law practice were all factors in my decision to stay in Denver. I also got very good advice from my friend, former US Senator Tim Wirth, who counseled against any Washington agency position. He warned—correctly—that I would be a target for the bureaucrats and regarded as a Clinton informant.

In July, after the tumult of manufactured scandals like Whitewater, Travelgate and Filegate, my friend and Deputy White House Counsel Vince Foster committed suicide and stunned us all. He had been a steady and supportive friend to me in my time in Little Rock during the campaign and the transition. Vince and I had grown close and frequently consulted on issues that arose. He, too, was a Fellow of the American College of Trial Lawyers, and our professional backgrounds had much in common. He was a law partner of Hillary and her close friend. The two of them had referred cases to my firm, and I had referred matters to them at the Rose Law Firm. He also had grown up in Hope, Arkansas, and had been friends with Bill Clinton since childhood.

A courtly and consummate lawyer from outside DC, his relationship with both Clintons made him an easy target. He was constantly hectored and personally attacked by conservative Republicans, the *Wall Street*

Journal, and the gargoyles in the right-wing press. Suffering in silence from chronic and severe depression, he was finally overwhelmed and took his life in a park just outside Washington. His call records later showed that my invitation for dinner later that week was the last message he received. Upon learning of his death in a call from Bruce Lindsey, I flew to Washington and then joined the Clinton party at his funeral in Little Rock and burial in Hope. It was an overwhelming tragedy for Vince's family and all of his friends. Returning from his funeral in Arkansas as a sad and stunned guest on Air Force One, I steeled my resolve to stay out of Washington and its destructive atmosphere.

In the early fall, however, Kevin O'Keefe, now serving as deputy director of Presidential Personnel, called with a "Godfather offer"—one I could not refuse. The President would like me to accept his appointment as the "Irish observer"; that is, the US Observer to the International Fund for Ireland. The position was to be filled by a private citizen who would serve as the President's personal representative to the board of the IFI, a multinational, foundation-like entity jointly operated by the Irish and British governments. The IFI, established as part of the Anglo-Irish Agreement discussed earlier, had been recognized and initially funded by the US Congress. The IFI's principal purpose was to promote peace, reconciliation, and economic development in Northern Ireland and the six border counties of the Republic of Ireland. Primarily funded by the United States and the European Union with other contributions from the governments of Canada, New Zealand, and Australia in recognition of their Irish communities, the IFI budget was some $40 million per year and was directed to cross-community redevelopment and regeneration projects in this designated twelve-county area on the island.

After doing my due diligence, I accepted. I was confident that my background in community banking, law, and my lifelong study of Irish history and politics would serve me well. Also, I am 100 percent ethnic Irish, my mother being descended from Protestants in the north and my father from Catholics in the south—a fact, I later learned, that was not lost on the White House. So, in November 1993, equipped with a new US diplomatic passport, my own thick research binder, and briefings from the National Security Council, I went to Ireland for my first IFI board meeting.

At the same time, events were in motion that would change Ireland forever. Gerry Adams, leader of Sinn Fein, and John Hume, leader of the moderate SDLP, had agreed to combine nationalism forces to press for a political solution to the Troubles. This formed part of the foundation that led to the Downing Street Declaration by Prime Minister John Major of Great Britain and Albert Reynolds, *Taoiseach* (prime minister) of the Republic of Ireland. At its essence, the Declaration pronounced the principle that the people of Ireland, north and south, had the exclusive right to solve their issues by mutual consent. It pledged the two governments to seek a constitutional solution with all political parties willing to forswear violence. The Declaration and the talks between Gerry Adams and John Hume led to an IRA ceasefire, followed shortly thereafter by an announced ceasefire by loyalist paramilitaries. And so, by early 1994, I found myself at the center of this complex and vexing swirl of events.

Chapter Four

The Beginnings in Belfast

Arriving for the first time in the dark and rainy Belfast winter, I could hardly imagine that I would come to regard Belfast as a second home. Over the coming years, I would become intimately familiar with this charming, red-bricked, and beautiful city of about three hundred thousand people with well-kept neighborhoods, English gardens, and public parks. I would also become intimately familiar with the so-called disadvantaged areas—the hard, battle zone–like neighborhoods where sectarianism, joblessness, and violence had ruled for so long.

Belfast is a monument to the Victorian age and the might that was the Industrial Revolution and the British Empire. From the time of the Norman Conquest, Belfast grew from a local settlement on the River Lagan to a mercantile center for the surrounding farms and lands. In the seventeenth century, Belfast became an established town initially settled by English and Scottish immigrants as part of the Ulster Plantation.

In the eighteenth and nineteenth centuries, Belfast entered its golden age. Shipping and the linen and ship-building industries flourished; the *Titanic* and its sister ships were built here. The city grew and prospered and, for a time, was larger than Dublin. Cultural amenities like the Linen Hall Library, the Opera House, and grand public buildings were constructed and still grace the downtown area. However, Protestant culture dominated the city and its politics while resentment among Catholics grew amid blatant discrimination in housing, employment, and education. Periodically, these tensions would boil over, and after Bloody Sunday in Derry in 1972 and the birth of the Troubles, Belfast was ground zero.

The city is divided into distinct neighborhoods radiating from the city center. From the majestic and ornate Georgian-style City Hall at the center of the city, Belfast (Irish for "river crossing") unfolds to the east across the Lagan River, past the once mighty Harland & Wolff shipyards with nearby neighborhoods like Short Strand, to the leafy green suburbs of Stormont, Hollywood, and Bangor along the coast. To the north lie neighborhoods like the Ardoyne and Castlereagh, working- and middle-class enclaves where Catholics and Protestants live in mixed and volatile surroundings. To the west, running up to Black Mountain, is notorious West Belfast and its divided sectarian turf: the Falls, the upper and lower Shankill, Springvale, and Springfield Road—all bound together in a history of bullets and bombs. To the south, past Sandy Row ("where the Catholics don't go") and further on along the Malone Road, lies the bucolic campus of Queens University (founded by Victoria herself), the Botanic Gardens, and large, stately homes of the upper- and middle-class academics and professionals. In time, I would come to know them all and see in each of them what Yeats meant by "the terrible beauty" that is Ireland.

West Belfast

Leaving central Belfast, one crosses the motorway and enters West Belfast. A short drive of about ten minutes, it is a journey "through the looking glass" from a bustling and prosperous downtown to a patchwork quilt of divided neighborhoods, painted curbstones that mark territory, and brick walls and concertina wire that make up "the peace line." It is perhaps the most dangerous territory in the United Kingdom but also one where, amidst the army patrols and screaming sectarian murals, uniformed schoolchildren walk to their classrooms and playgrounds, women go to market, and shops and pubs are open for the business of daily life.

But everywhere a palpable tension permeates the atmosphere, and you know you are in a place that could erupt at any time, day or night. In some ways, it's as if you've left downtown Los Angeles and found your way into East LA or Watts, with sectarian murals replacing gang graffiti.

Amidst the checkerboard of nationalist and loyalist neighborhoods, often divided by no more than a few feet of brick wall and concertina wire, each community has struggled to maintain itself and provide support and hope for a better future. These efforts are often housed in the abandoned factories, textile mills, and small storefront offices of community partnerships and organizations like the Upper Springfield Development Trust, the Greater Shankill Partnership, and the Flax Trust. And in these small, cramped spaces are found some of the most remarkable and courageous people in Northern Ireland and maybe in the world.

The Upper Springfield Development Trust

Geraldine McAteer was born and raised in the nationalist Catholic neighborhood on the Upper Springfield Road, at the far end of West Belfast at the foot of Black Mountain. An attractive and engaging woman then in her forties, she has survived poverty, divorce, sectarian violence, and life-long discrimination. Her father and brother were both victims of such violence, as have been other members of the Springfield community—men, women, and children. In 1998, a close associate and aide, Terry Enright, was shot to death in a sectarian murder. Nonetheless, this remarkable woman continues to bring her own strength and perseverance to the service of her community through the Upper Springfield Development Trust (USDT).

The USDT that she cofounded operates on government-provided funding, private contributions, and grants from organizations like the IFI. It provides job counseling, placement services, and computer training for young men and women seeking employment in the burgeoning software industry in Belfast. Always in need of more and better funding, USDT operates from a storefront location in a strip mall surrounded by tidy but small red brick public housing units in this nationalist enclave or "estate."

Realizing the future of her constituents lies beyond the boundaries of their neighborhood, Geraldine has reached out to the American software industry and formed personal alliances with successful software entrepreneurs like John Cullinane of Boston and his colleague in Belfast, American expat and Irish historian Dr. Frank Costello. With the help of John and the IFI, these alliances have led to the founding of software call centers that have provided scores of jobs for the men and women trained at the USDT.

John and Frank were also instrumental in founding the Friends of Belfast with the Belfast City Council. The Friends is a network created to promote Belfast business opportunities in cities in the United States, starting with their home town of Boston and in Pittsburgh, home to a substantial and active Irish American community. The Pittsburgh Irish American community was led by Tony O'Reilly, former chairman and CEO of H. J. Heinz Company; Dan Rooney Sr., owner of the Pittsburgh Steelers (and later US ambassador to Ireland); Mayor Tom Murphy; and the late Sister Michelle O'Leary, head of the Irish Institute of the University of Pittsburgh. But success in Belfast is often measured in inches, and hard-fought ground can be quickly lost.

Geraldine was one of the first IFI project leaders I visited and later came to know well. Her dedication to her constituents was evident from the first day. She was a classic example of the strong women in both Northern Ireland communities who have persevered in the cause of non-violence and cross-community regeneration. These women leaders were an essential part of the foundation on which the peace process was built and eventually succeeded. Perhaps not as well known outside Northern Ireland as Nobel laureates Mairead Corrigan Maguire and Betty Williams, women like Geraldine in the nationalist community and May Blood (now Baroness Blood) in the loyalist community worked unsung for years across sectarian lines to bring jobs and dignity to the communities, end the violence, and return safety and a future to their working-class neighborhoods.

In addition to her work with the USDT, Geraldine is an organizer of events in the Falls Road community that promote its unique culture and history and the Irish language. A former church on the Falls now serves as a community center, coffee shop, bookstore, and gathering place for the Falls community. It is also the center of the annual West Belfast Festival in August, one of the largest in Europe, which showcases the people, music, art, food, and crafts of the Falls. The festival has brought tourism and economic benefit to the Falls, as well as a greater sense of community, pride, and promise.

The Greater Shankill Partnership

East down the Springfield Road and back toward town center is the loyalist neighborhood simply known as the Shankill. Named for the (Upper and Lower) Shankill Road that is its heart, the Shankill was home to some of the bloodiest and continuing violence in the province. It is also the home of the Greater Shankill Partnership and its founder and driving force, Jackie Redpath.

Jackie Redpath is a small, wiry man then in his late forties. He bears a striking resemblance to rocker Rod Stewart. With a shock of red hair, a quick and nervous demeanor, and an ever present cigarette, he is a well-spoken and thoughtful product of this fiercely loyalist community. Unlike many of his community and his generation, Jackie did not seek his future in the mills or shipyards as an apprentice to a father, uncle, or other relative. Rather, realizing the limitations of the apprentice system and the importance of education, he went on to study social work and community regeneration at Queens and returned to the Shankill after graduation to help build a brighter and better place.

Like the USDT, the Greater Shankill Partnership (GSP) is an organization dedicated to community improvement, cross-community cooperation, and job training and counseling. GSP is likewise funded by government grants and organizations like the IFI. Its programs reach across the Shankill area and include sports, health and wellness, and neighborhood renewal. GSP also operates the Spectrum Centre, which is an arts and culture venue in the heart of the Shankill.

Located near the Brown Bear pub once used as the headquarters of the notorious "Shankill Butchers," the GSP stands as an outpost in a shrinking loyalist community that feels abandoned, isolated, and betrayed. In the summer of 1999, the Shankill was the scene of bloody turf warfare between competing loyalist gangs. Homes were burned and firebombed, and scores of families who had lived for generations in the neighborhood were left homeless or forced to flee to safer ground.

Over the years, Jackie and I, like Geraldine and I, developed a working relationship through the IFI and then a friendship based on respect and trust.

Visiting one would always have me visit the other in order to ensure that both viewpoints were heard and communicated to the Clinton White House. Mostly, I listened to them—sometimes separately but often together—as they shared a common commitment as well as great respect for each other. Indeed, during the worst of the paramilitary gang wars on the Shankill during the summer of 1999, Geraldine offered her own home as a refuge to Jackie, his wife, and his sons, as he was in constant danger trying to be a peacemaker and caught in the middle between two violent factions of loyalism. (Jackie declined the offer to stay at her home but sent his family out of the area.)

Today there is stability on the Shankill (and Jackie is trying to smoke a little less). But the smoldering fears and suspicions that fester beneath the surface on the Falls and on the Shankill remain; these forces are kept in check by the personal dedication and courage of men and women working on the streets, day in and day out—men and women like Geraldine McAteer and Jackie Redpath.

The Ardoyne

To the north of West Belfast and slightly across town lies north Belfast, and on the Crumlin Road is the neighborhood known as the Ardoyne. Home to Catholics and Protestants alike, the Ardoyne had its heyday in the late nineteenth and early twentieth centuries as home to numerous textile factories and linen mills. These factories and mills provided employment mostly for women workers who soaked the flax, extracted the fiber, and spun the yarn that became Irish linen, the world standard. Working all day in drafty, unheated spaces, barefoot (to save their shoes) in freezing, ankle-deep water used to process the flax, these women were generally the sole support of the family. Brutal working conditions took their toll; crippled by arthritis and poor health, few lasted beyond their forties. Young women, desperate to make some income, readily took their places and eventually suffered the same fate. Over the generations, their bare feet wore down the stone steps, which are all that's left to mark their passing.

Today these mills and factories are gone or empty, gray and long-broken buildings, hulking mausoleums to textile competition, changing world markets, and cheaper Third World labor. All, that is, but one: the old Brookfield Mill, home of the Brookfield Business Centre and the Flax Trust.

Built in the 1850s, Brookfield Mill (and its sister mill, Rosebank) is a multi-story granite fortress where flax was turned into linen. Here, women soaked the plants, stripped the flax, and fed it into huge, noisy presses and dangerous spinning machines. In a laborious process, linen cloth was made over several factory floors joined by stone stairwells down which flowed a steady stream of cold water. Vacant for decades, Brookfield came to life again during the worst of the Troubles of the 1970s.

The rebirth of Brookfield was the vision of one man, a young Catholic parish priest named Myles Kavanagh. Assigned to Holy Cross Parish, he could look every day down the hill to the hulking silence of the Brookfield Mill and the past prosperity it had represented for this bitterly divided community. Repeated attacks on the church and rectory—including a bomb that blew him out of bed and the stained glass out of the church windows—caused him to consider what could be done to end the violence. Slowly a vision emerged: a community resource center that could incubate small businesses in the hulking Brookfield Mill, provide outreach, offer job counseling and training, and be a "safe space" to grow ideas and opportunities, just like flax was made into linen. With some small government assistance and private contributions from Irish Americans like Dan Rooney of the Pittsburgh Steelers and Bill Flynn of New York–based Mutual of America, Kavanagh set out to reshape this community and rebuild a shattered neighborhood.

Myles Kavanagh is charismatic, mischievous, and indefatigably optimistic—in short, a true Irishman. He is a master salesman with a quick laugh and self-deprecating sense of humor. He is also fearless—both for his own safety and in pursuit of his dream for the Flax Trust and the Brookfield Mill. In the late seventies, a young woman knocked on his parish rectory door and offered to join his cause. She was a Palentine nun named Mary Turley. Born in the Republic of Ireland, she felt compelled to be on the front lines of the Troubles. She received the permission of her order to explore working with Father Myles. She has been there ever since.

Myles is larger than life, outgoing, and exuberant; Sister Mary is quiet, studious, and never misses a detail. The result was and is a legendary partnership. Together, they built the Flax Trust into an international institution. Its annual gala in Belfast, its dinner and fundraiser in New

York, and its honors breakfast in Washington, DC, are compulsory events for the Belfast business community and the Irish American business and political communities.

Over thirty years later, the Flax Trust is a model for small-business incubation and a haven and resource for both communities. In addition, the trust operates UCIT, the Ulster Community Investment Trust. Originally created and funded by the IFI, UCIT provides funds to other community organizations and partnerships in anticipation of government grants and the repayment of loans to development projects.

The Brookfield Business Centre is now home to a number of small businesses, craftsmen and artisans, and job counseling facilities. It also leases space to sophisticated Internet/web businesses as well as offering computer training. On the grounds is a dormitory for young people in training, an art gallery, and a community theater. Also on the grounds is a pub and restaurant called the Pittsburgh Steeler (in deference to Dan Rooney and his family) where the annual Super Bowl party is the neighborhood event of the drab Belfast winter.

But, as in West Belfast, sectarian ugliness is always simmering in the Ardoyne. In the summer of 2001, it bubbled up from its sewer at Holy Cross School. Vicious loyalist thugs targeted a short street leading to the school and taunted, threatened, and attacked terrified Catholic primary school children and their parents. Army units and RUC security were called in, and eventually the outburst faded away—but not until another generation of children had been scarred for life with the memory and terror of their neighbors' viciously expressed sectarian hatred.

In December 2002, I visited the school with Father Myles, who is still the school's chaplain. The soldiers, police, and thugs were gone as I talked with the principal, several parents, and their daughters. In their eyes, I saw relief and a return to school routine. But I also saw a sad resignation over the fact that this could happen again and that a handful of ignorant louts on one hundred feet of street could terrorize a community and shock a watching world. Such still is life in the Ardoyne.

East Belfast

On the east side of the Lagan River, east of downtown on the other side of Belfast, by the Harland & Wolff shipyards and miles from the leafy green enclaves of Stormont and Hollywood, lie the working-class, largely Protestant neighborhoods of East Belfast. This is the home turf of demagogue Ian Paisley and his Democratic Ulster Party. But here, too, community leadership has overcome political obstacles and contributed to economic improvement and cross-community understanding. The key organization is the East Belfast Partnership, and its founder, director, and guiding light is Sammy Douglas.

Sammy is a small, stout, white-haired man then in his late forties. He speaks quietly and quickly with a thick Ulster Scot's brogue that sometimes escapes the American ear. He is invariably upbeat, warm, and quick to laugh, belying the fact that he, too, is in constant danger and regarded by some as a "sellout" to loyalism.

Like the Upper Springfield Development Trust, the Greater Shankill Partnership, and the Brookfield Business Centre, the East Belfast Partnership (EBP) provides job counseling and training and a business incubator (which President Clinton and I called on during his first Belfast visit in December 1995). Also, the East Belfast Partnership reaches across community lines and provides needed services and resources for the adjoining Catholic enclave in the area, the Short Strand. And, like the annual Falls Road summer art and folk festival in West Belfast, the EBP has looked to its own resources and created an interactive website. The site promotes East Belfast in lively music and video as a business opportunity and tourist destination, showcasing the shops, pubs, and sectarian mural art. On behalf of the administration, I was privileged to launch the site from the steps of Stormont in 1999.

Geraldine, Jackie, May Blood, Father Myles, Sister Mary, Sammy— and others like them and those who will follow in their footsteps—have proven the critical importance of community leaders on the ground and that cross-community cooperation can build a better Belfast for all. At great sacrifice, and often at personal risk, they are defining the future of Belfast and the province itself.

Chapter Five

The Ex-Con and the Mother

Two of the most memorable and important figures in my experiences in Northern Ireland are unknown to each other but bound together by violent death and indomitable will. One is a convicted loyalist killer, the other a grieving Catholic mother.

Billy Hutchinson

Billy Hutchinson is a thin, angular man then in his forties who runs ten miles a day, every day, regardless of weather. He is soft spoken and devoted to his family. He served as a Belfast City Councilor and is a member of the Northern Ireland Assembly. He and his colleague, the late David Ervine, were the leaders of the PUP, a unionist party that is the political representative of the loyalist UDA. Billy is also a convicted killer.

In October 1974, Hutchinson, a member of the UDA, was involved in the drive-by killing of two young Catholic men in Belfast. The victims were unknown to Hutchinson and were selected at random as a target for sectarian retaliation. Hutchinson was apprehended, tried, convicted, and sentenced to life in prison. After serving almost twenty years, he was paroled and returned to the streets of Belfast, having spent his twenties and thirties in a British maximum-security prison.

I first met Hutchinson in 1993 when I visited an ex-prisoners' program being run by Hutchinson and an ex-IRA gunman named Tommy O'Gorman. Like Hutchinson, O'Gorman had served twenty or so years of a life sentence for murder and had been paroled under programs designed to allow rehabilitated prisoners to return to the community. Each had had an epiphany in prison and had committed himself to working with other ex-prisoners to reintegrate into society and lead productive, nonviolent lives. The program they ran was on the western fringe of West Belfast at the foot of Black Mountain in a structure that once served as a maintenance building for a city park. Here, the two of them worked with ex-prisoners looking to find scarce jobs and a new and constructive purpose for their lives.

Over the coming years, Hutchinson and I developed a relationship, in part based on our mutual interest in running. On my visits to Belfast, I would contact Billy and run a few miles with him in the darkness of early morning. Pounding through the quiet streets of Belfast, we would talk about current conditions—political, social, and economic—as he saw them from his unique perspective on the ground within the loyalist communities. Although some saw him as a turncoat, Billy was generally respected by this community to which he had literally given so much of his life. He was dedicated to seeing that they would not be left out of the political mix and economic opportunity. Our conversations were always candid and off the record, but he knew that his views were important to us and would be fairly and seriously considered. I came to regard Billy and the late David Ervine (also a loyalist ex-prisoner) as reliable and reasonable voices for this constituency, which included some of the hardest and most intransigent elements of loyalism. I respected their leadership and admired their personal courage. Without them, a key element of this community, often thought to be intractable, would never have joined the peace process. Without them, the Good Friday Agreement and its institutions would never have had a chance to get off the ground.

After the Good Friday Agreement and his election to Stormont as a member of the new local assembly, Billy and I saw less of each other but still managed to run together on occasion. Sometimes, unexpectedly, he would cancel or not appear out of the predawn murkiness in front of my hotel. I would later read or learn that he was under yet another death threat and didn't think it was safe for me to be with him. So he would run a different route, alone and exposed, rain or shine, day in and day out.

One February morning, we met in the dark outside the venerable Europa Hotel. Located in downtown Belfast, the Europa was once the most-bombed hotel in Europe. However, when IFI money and US guests made it off limits, the Europa and its large lounge area/bar on the mezzanine floor became a salon for both business and politics for all sides.

On this forbidding morning, the rain and sleet were coming down in sheets, and the wind seemed near gale force off the Irish sea. I suggested we pass on the run and have some breakfast instead, but Billy was having none of it. As we headed off toward Sandy Row, I asked him why he put himself through this routine every day. He said he assumed that I had never been in prison.

"No, I haven't," I told him.

"Well," he said, "I have. I promised myself that if I ever got outside those walls and got another chance at life, I'd never miss a day. This is my promise, and I won't break it."

Billy remains a spokesman and leader for his loyalist community. He continues to serve their interests in the Assembly and the political community at large. In addition to serving an important role in the run up to the Good Friday Agreement and thereafter, he stands out as someone who can change his life and serve his community with skill and honor.

Margaret McKinney and the "Messenger from God"

Margaret McKinney is a petite, white-haired woman with sparklingly clear blue eyes. In her sixties when we first met, she smiles readily and with warmth that belies her life for the last twenty years. Margaret McKinney is the mother of a dead son, one of the "disappeared" taken by the IRA and never heard from again. Hers has been a life of daily anguish.

I first met Margaret in the Roosevelt Room in the White House during St. Patrick's Day events in March 1995. She was sitting with a small group of women from Northern Ireland waiting for an audience with the Clintons. Her group, WAVE (Women Against Violence Empowered), was seeking the endorsement of the President and First Lady for their organization composed of women who had lost loved ones to the violence. I introduced myself to them and happened to sit down next to Margaret. We chatted while we waited, and she told me her story. Her son was one of "the disappeared," men and women who, for one transgression or another, real or contrived, had been taken by the IRA and never heard from again. The list included ordinary citizens, petty criminals, informers, and, in one case (Jean McConville), a mother of ten young children.

Showing me yellowed newspaper articles, she told me of her son Brian, the middle of her three children. Moderately retarded and in his late teens, Brian had finally found his first job, as a janitor. He was filled with the pride and dignity that employment and a small wage gave him. One day after work, some other boys in the Catholic neighborhood where they lived put Brian up to a "joke." Using what he thought was a toy gun, he was to "scare" a local shopkeeper and take the money from the till. He was assured that it was all in good fun, the shopkeeper was in on the prank, and no one would get hurt. Trusting his newfound friends, and no doubt seeking acceptance, he did just that. He returned home to share the "joke" with his parents. Shocked, they took him and the money back to the shopkeeper and made Brian apologize. Knowing Brian's condition and the family, the shopkeeper agreed not to press charges and let the matter end.

Later that night, several men in balaclavas broke into the McKinney home and dragged Brian off. IRA self-styled vigilantes, they told the family that Brian needed to be warned off further wrongdoing but that he would be returned unharmed "in a few days." He never came back. Frantic, the McKinneys begged the IRA for their son's return. They received no response. As days turned to weeks, weeks to months, and months to years, the McKinneys came to accept that Brian was dead. Now all they wanted was his remains so he could have a proper burial and they could have peace. Finishing her story, Margaret asked if I could help find her son.

My own family had suffered the loss of my youngest brother at age sixteen in a car accident. I had seen and knew all too well the devastation that parents suffer and the wound to the soul that never heals from the loss of a child. I agreed to do what I could. We went to the Oval Office, and I had Margaret repeat her story for the Clintons. Listening intently, they were both visibly moved. Later, speaking privately with the President,

I asked for and instantly received his approval to help this woman find her son.

The only help available was an expression of personal interest "from the highest levels of the White House" and pressure on Sinn Fein, the political representative of the IRA. So I began such a campaign, with persistent calls, conversations, and notes to the Sinn Fein leadership, Gerry Adams, Martin McGuinness, and Gerry Kelly. I let no appropriate opportunity pass without raising Brian McKinney with them. Although they were sympathetic, they pointed out the difficulties: the passage of time, the lack of records, the unknown identity of the killers, and the like. My message in return was simple: keep trying; this is an opportunity for the IRA to do the right thing—a political win/win. I was assured that they were doing their best; my answer was, "Do better."

In the meantime, I developed a warm relationship with the McKinney family. We corresponded regularly, and Margaret often sent me cards and prayers for me and my family. I would visit her tidy, small home off the Upper Springfield Road for tea and conversation whenever my Belfast schedule permitted. I wanted her to know her cause was not forgotten.

Through several false alarms and dashed hopes, Margaret kept her faith that we would find Brian. And, eventually, in the fall of 1998, a tip led to a remote field in County Monaghan across the border and to Brian's body, still wearing his "wee blue tennis shoes." A dignified funeral was held, and Brian was laid to rest in a cemetery a few blocks from his parents' home.

Margaret has continued her activism in the cause of nonviolence. She has traveled to Europe, Africa, and America to tell her story and promote the role of women and mothers as peacemakers in divided societies. She has written of her experience and wrote that I was "a messenger sent to her by God." She prays the rosary every day and tells me that I am always "on her beads."

Margaret McKinney's is not an isolated story. Hundreds of Northern Ireland mothers—Catholic and Protestant—have suffered the loss of or injury to loved ones, picked through rubble to find or identify body parts, and dealt with maimed and crippled husbands, sons, daughters, and grandchildren. Yet, somehow, they have persevered through each day, hope coexisting with anguish and pain. Margaret and those suffering mothers are a testament to the strength and power of a mother's love and devotion but also personify the unyielding will of the women of Northern Ireland to find peace and reconciliation. In the end, they will surely triumph.

Chapter Six

Derry

Derry (or formally Londonderry) is said to be the last surviving medieval-style walled city in Europe. It sits proudly on an island where the Foyle River joins the Irish Sea and forms a deepwater port. It is the principal city in "the West," that portion of Northern Ireland west of the Bann River. This rural region is rugged, hilly, and generally has a poorer quality of farmland. It is predominantly Catholic.

During World War II, the US Navy had a substantial presence in Derry because of this port and access to the sea. At the end of the war, the remnants of the German U-boat fleet chose to surrender here to the Allies. The subs were sunk in the deep water and now form artificial reefs for sea life.

Tradition has it that the original settlement, Doire (meaning "oak grove"), was built by the monk Colmcille on the site of an ancient Druid sacred oak grove. It is also said that he cut down the grove, which, if true, is the first recorded act of religious violence in Ireland.

The city itself is nothing less than a magnificent trip back to a medieval time. Thick stone walls punctuated by ancient portals or gates mark this citadel and capital of the Donegal region. Originally a Catholic stronghold due to its charter from King James in 1662, Derry has a sizeable Protestant population that annually celebrates the victory of the Apprentice Boys over the city besieged by forces of the Jacobites in the seventeenth century.

Catholics were expelled from the city and relegated to a swampy area outside the walls known as the Bogside.

For the next three centuries, Protestants maintained control of the city, its economy, and its government until the civil rights struggles in the late 1960s. And, in January 1972, it was here that Bloody Sunday took place. On that fateful Sunday, a civil rights march turned horrific when British paratroopers—falsely believing themselves to have been fired upon—opened up with automatic weapons into the unarmed crowd. Thirteen people were killed and scores wounded, including a priest seeking to aid the injured while waving a white handkerchief. The nationalist community was inflamed, the IRA reborn, and the modern Troubles begun. "Free Derry" was born on the site, and sectarian murals marked nationalist territory, off limits to police and the army.

In the next several years, Derry would pay a horrific price in blood and buildings. Virtually every block in old, central Derry was either destroyed or bombed into dereliction.

Much has been written about the causes and events of Bloody Sunday. Indeed, a British tribunal probed the death of the thirteen and the wounding of the others but did not issue its report until June 2010. Thereafter, British Prime Minister David Cameron finally apologized on behalf of the British government, and some compensation to victims and their families has been paid. But no one can come to Derry or hope to understand it or its people without coming to grips with the legacy of that awful day and how the good people of Derry—from both communities—work tirelessly to overcome it and rebuild their community.

Numerous initiatives have been undertaken to help rebuild the economy and provide much-needed jobs to the area. The Derry Partnership, supported by the local business community, has reached across the Atlantic to attract quality call centers to the area, and the Port of Boston, Massachusetts, has been actively working with the port of Derry to renovate, modernize, and promote its port facilities and regional airport. Tourism in Derry and the lush surrounding Donegal countryside is once again a factor in the city's growing vibrancy.

When one arrives in Derry from the east and crosses the Foyle into the town center, a large statue of two men dominates the roundabout. They are larger than life, and each is extending his hand to the other, but the hands do not quite touch. It is called "Hands Across the Divide" (see the book's cover) and symbolizes Derry today: a community striving to overcome past differences and wrongs while looking to a better common future based on justice and mutual respect. In the words of John Hume, Derry's native son and Nobel laureate, "we must learn to spill our sweat, not our blood." For many, this has become the city's call to a new kind of arms. For me, the story of Derry is again the story of special places and extraordinary people in the community who dedicated themselves to peace, reconciliation, and prosperity. It is also the land of my paternal ancestors, the clan Dougherty. Several Derryites loom large and will forever mark my Derry experience. Among them are Paddy Doherty, John and Pat Hume, Reggie and Phil Ryan, Phil Coulter, and Willie McCarter.

Paddy Doherty

One of the most recognizable and colorful figures in Derry is a small, white-haired dynamo in his seventies, Paddy Doherty, or as he is known throughout a town full of Dohertys, O'Doghertys, and Doughertys, "Paddy Bogside." A lifelong resident of the hardscrabble Catholic ghetto in the western shadow of the Derry walls, Doherty is a self-educated man who has been a carpenter, plumber, brick mason, and jack of all building trades. Father of eight children, he has played a leadership role for decades in the civil rights struggles of the Catholic community in Derry, earning the unofficial title of "Mayor of the Bogside." Everyone in Derry knows Paddy Bogside.

In the height of the Troubles, Paddy set his sights and formidable energies on economic regeneration. He is the founder and guiding light behind the Derry Inner City Trust, the Calgach Centre, and a new hotel at Magazine Gate on the west side of the old walled city.

The Inner City Trust undertook the daunting task of organizing and funding much of the reconstruction of the core city of Derry. Beautiful old structures, townhomes, and quaint shops were destroyed or damaged by bombs and fires during the Troubles of the seventies. Indeed, pictures of the time show a Derry that looks like London during the Blitz. Often working with his own hands and tools, Paddy led the effort to rebuild Derry and shape its economic future. Eventually supported by government grant, the IFI, and leaders from both communities, the Inner City Trust accomplished nothing less than the restoration of the core of Derry within its old and historic walls.

But Doherty did not stop there. Sensing that the future lies in recognition of shared heritage and origins, he envisioned a unique attraction for natives and tourists alike, the Calgach Centre. Named for a mythical Celtic leader of ancient times, the Calgach Centre is a multistory facility that offers community meeting facilities, a cafeteria, a visitor's center, and an audiovisual experience called "The Fifth Province." "The Fifth Province" transports the visitor across millennia of Irish history from the ancient pre-Celtic time to the future. It is an attraction of Disney quality and takes the visitor, riding in a "time machine," to "the Fifth Irish Province," the province of the mind and the imagination. It is a unique experience and a powerful reminder that all in Derry share a common and proud Celtic origin and are bound together for the future.

Across the narrow, cobblestoned street from the center at Magazine Gate is the site of Derry's newest hotel, another longtime vision of Paddy Bogside. Opened a few years ago, the hotel was in a race with Doherty, who was suffering from cancer. But Paddy Bogside once again defied the odds and opened that hotel. Unfortunately, we missed each other on my last trip—he was on his way to South Africa for Habitat for Humanity. But as I showed my daughter through the revitalized ancient town, I felt his spirit permeate and energize old Derry and the Bogside, whether he was there or not.

Glen Barr and the Waterside

Across the center of old Derry, on the east side of the Foyle River, sits the Protestant community known as the Waterside. Here, on hills that overlook the city and the broad river, are the homes, shops, and businesses of this middle-class Protestant community. And here also is located the working dream of one of its leaders, Glen Barr.

The Maydown Ebrington Centre is located in a refurbished small mill that once housed one of Derry's many world-famous shirt factories. Abandoned for years, the building has been transformed into a complex that includes a state-of-the-art community theater, a restaurant, and offices. It also houses youth counseling services and a computer training center that equips its largely female graduates to work for the several call and service centers that have located in the Derry area.

But the success of Maydown is not the end of Barr's vision. Rather, he has tirelessly promoted—and has now seen come to reality—a battlefield memorial and peace studies center near Ypres, Belgium. There, during World War I and the bloody battle of the Somme, regiments of Irish Protestants (Thirty-Sixth Ulster) and Catholics (Sixteenth Irish), for the first and only time, fought, bled, and died side by side in the Allied cause. This remarkable event, symbolizing cross-community brotherhood in common cause, has served as a powerful metaphor for this community and how Barr sees Derry's past and future.

It has not been an easy journey for Barr. A stocky man then in his late forties, he is a veteran of the merchant marines. He later became president of its union and an outspoken leader of the loyalist UDA/UVF. He served in Stormont during the seventies and was a member of the hard-core Unionist "Vanguard," along with David Trimble, Northern Ireland's original first minister. But slowly he, like Trimble, realized that bridges must be built across the religious divide. Leaving politics, he returned to his community, and the Maydown concept was born.

Over lunch, we renewed our relationship and recollected how trust and respect formed the foundation of cross-community progress. In fact, that very day, the Orange Orders were parading through Derry in commemoration of the ouster of its seventeenth-century mayor, who had threatened to unlock the city gates to the invading Catholic forces of King James. The parade is traditionally held on December 16, but the Orders had been asked by local businessmen and women—Catholic and Protestant—to march earlier in the month and not disrupt the Christmas shopping season. The Orders agreed, and the parades went off without a hitch—a small but important compromise that shows again the promise of a better day in Derry.

John Hume, Reggie Ryan, and Phil Coulter: the Friends

Three men and friends from childhood in Derry—A Noble laureate, a world-famous songwriter/entertainer, and a renowned restaurateur—form an enduring chapter in my Derry experiences. Their stories and lives all orbit within the powerful gravity that is Derry.

John Hume is from a large Catholic family raised in the Bogside. Poor but very bright, he received a scholarship that made an otherwise unattainable university education possible. Returning to Derry, he taught high school French and was the founder of the successful credit union movement. But he could not help but get caught up in the civil rights movement of the sixties, including Bloody Sunday. Joining other young leaders, Hume rose to form the moderate Catholic party, the SDLP, and went on to become a member of the British Parliament and the European Parliament, an international figure, and a tireless supporter of economic development for his beloved Derry. John conceived and promoted the Derry Partnership, which successfully sought transatlantic business links for Derry. Companies like Stream, Seagate, and DuPont found the opportunity compelling and operate successful facilities in Derry.

A lover of red wine and a gifted singer of Irish ballads, Hume, along with his key allies, Seamus Mallon and Mark Durkan, forged a government partnership with the UUP led by David Trimble (his co-Nobel laureate) and Sir Reg Empey. Together, they created the coalition government that initially operated Northern Ireland in fulfillment of the Good Friday Agreement.

John and his wife, Pat, raised a family amidst all the political turmoil and violence that was the Troubles. With Pat's tireless support, love, and understanding, John served in the British Parliament, the Parliament of the European Union, and the Stormont Local Assembly—all while making countless trips to Europe and the United States in search of inward investment for Derry and Northern Ireland. For all his contributions, he has been recognized with the Nobel Peace Prize (with David Trimble), the Gandhi Peace Prize, and the Martin Luther King Peace Award—the only person to have been recognized with all three honors.

John and Pat became our good friends, and Marcia and I were pleased to host them at our home in Denver when he spoke as part of the Nobel Laureates program at Regis University. David Trimble similarly accepted a later invitation from us and spoke at Regis as well. Both men were well received and brought their unique perspectives and examples of exceptional courage to rapt audiences.

Reggie Ryan is a soft-spoken and gracious man born and raised in Derry. A childhood friend of Hume and Coulter, Ryan tried his hand at various businesses, only to taste failure and sectarian violence. His last venture in Derry, a carpet business in the center of town, was bombed with only a moment's notice to him and his employees. Diving out the front door and under a sheltering truck with the explosion at his heels, Ryan decided it was time to find a new life. And he did. An accomplished amateur chef, Ryan determined to make a go of it in the restaurant business. Trying and failing at a fish and chips shop, he took a chance on a small country house in the nearby fishing village of Fahan, fifteen miles from Derry on Lough Swilly.

Reggie's inn sits on a hill with breathtaking views overlooking the Inch Island and the Swilly. The Lough (or simply the Swilly) divides Donegal from the Inishowen peninsula. It is a deep, wide, fjord-like estuary that leads to the Irish Sea. Home to the hardy sailors of Donegal, the Swilly has seen much history, including the Viking war ships that plundered the Irish coast; the Flight of the Earls, who were the last of the native Irish chieftains; and US submarines based in Derry during World War II. Fortifications from the Napoleonic era, when Great Britain prepared for a French invasion to support Irish rebels, still dot the cliffs and are visible from the long, sandy beaches (or "strands") that run along some of its gently sloping shores.

In the early eighties, a little-used summer house was offered for sale to him by its then owner, Phil Coulter, another friend from childhood. Today, with his wife and partner Philomena (known to all as Phil), the restaurant and small inn—St. John's—is perennially ranked as one of the best in Ireland. Many Irish American politicians have found their way to St. John's at one time or another: Senators Kennedy, Leahy, and Dodd were all guests.

For me, it was a frequent weekend hideaway from the exhausting and often gritty work in Belfast and Derry. My wife and children came to know it and love it as I did. I will long remember the special Donegal-style evenings, marked by wonderful meals fresh from local farms and the sea, great wine, and often spontaneous entertainment led by Phil Coulter on the piano and John Hume leading the rest of us in song. "Londonderry Aire" (also known as "Danny Boy") always rounded out the evenings.

Phil Coulter is now a world-famous, Grammy-nominated songwriter, pianist, and entertainer, known far and wide for his "Tranquility" songs and traditional Irish/Celtic music. Like Hume and Ryan, he is a product of Derry's poor Catholic community. He left Derry and eventually Ireland to seek his musical future in America, where he has won countless awards for his songs. But he has never forgotten who he is or where he comes from. His love song to Derry, "The Town I Knew So Well," has become its haunting anthem. It tells the story of the town in which he grew up, its transformation by sectarian violence and reconciliation and the hope for its future:

> For what's done is done, and what's won is won
> And what's lost is lost and gone forever
> I can only pray for a bright, brand new day
> In the town I loved so well.

(Copyright, Mews Music, author Phil Coulter)

It is known by all who love Derry and was emotionally sung by all on every St. Patrick's Day in the large White House parties during the Clinton years. And still, Coulter returns regularly to Derry to see old friends like Hume and Ryan and lend his voice and celebrity to the rebirth of his town and in support of cross-community reconciliation.

Watching these three old friends privately interact and reminisce together was always a welcome and rare privilege for me. It is an extraordinary glimpse into a bygone Derry that they all remember and love, despite the hardship and pain. Even though their youthful experiences were hard, none of them is bitter. In typical Irish fashion, they remember the good and the bad with equal measure of laughter and tears. But each man in his own way has risen above the discrimination, the hate, and the violence to realize his full talent and fulfillment. They are truly a model for those that come after them in a new Derry symbolized by its welcoming sculpture, "Hands Across the Divide."

Chapter Seven

Willie McCarter and the IFI

Since its creation in 1986 as part of the Anglo-Irish Agreement, the IFI (or "the Fund") has established itself as the major economic and community regeneration vehicle in Northern Ireland and the border counties of the Republic of Ireland. The IFI has employed a nonsectarian, cross-community philosophy that relies on its board of directors from the private sector, north and south, and observers from the donor countries to carry out its mission. The Fund's primary objective is to "prime the pump" of projects that create jobs, promote reconciliation, and underpin the peace process in communities and towns throughout the twelve counties.

In its early days, the IFI, like most innovations in Northern Ireland, was viewed with distrust and suspicion. Thought to be an instrument of a US policy that was perceived to be "green" (or nationalist), the Fund was initially shunned by the unionist and loyalist communities as "blood money." But over time and due to the nature of its cross-community performance and neutrality, the Fund became a vital part of the economic regeneration of the province. In no small measure, this is due to the work of one man, Willie McCarter, the chairman of the IFI from 1992 to 2003.

A short, stocky, white-bearded man, Willie is a hardy product of Donegal and his hometown of Buncrana, just north of Fahan on Lough Swilly. He and his brothers are the sons and nephews of the founders of McCarter & Sons, one of Ireland's largest and most successful textile mills. Acquired by Fruit of the Loom in the 1980s, the McCarter textile operation became one of the largest employers on the island and the largest cross-border employer. Providing at its peak more than two thousand jobs in three plants on both sides of the border, Fruit of the Loom was a model for inward investment and cross-community employment. Willie McCarter was head of European operations for Fruit of the Loom. We met when I joined the IFI Board in 1993 and he had just become Fund chairman.

Willie (as he is simply known all over the province) grew up in the textile business, taking time out only for university in London and an MBA from MIT. He is soft spoken, self-effacing, and devoted to the work of the Fund. From hardy Presbyterian Donegal stock and a veteran sailor of the open Irish Sea, he is a master at tacking against the wind and finding the "way forward." As well known as he is across the province, he is equally well known and respected in Dublin, London, and Washington.

The IFI under Willie's leadership has become an institution in Northern Ireland and a bold innovator of economic development. The Fund is operated through several established programs, including Wider Horizons, an exchange program to the United States for youth from both communities. Wider Horizons also sponsored the Jeanie Johnson Project, which was the construction of a full replica "coffin ship" of this name sailed across the Atlantic by trained young sailors from both communities for exhibition in the United States and Canada.

Other programs focus specifically on disadvantaged communities, providing direct funding to job programs or indirect funding through partnerships like the Upper Springfield Trust, the Greater Shankill Partnership, and the East Belfast Partnership.

Another program was RADIAN—Research and Development between Ireland and North America. This program was designed to match companies in the United States and Canada to similar companies in Northern Ireland to pursue mutual opportunities in both markets. The joint company projects were to be innovative, profitable, and market based. Initially, some eight ventures qualified; this grew to over thirty-four, of which thirty matured into substantive joint ventures for such things as ceramics, advanced electronics, trout farming, and offshore fishing net development. When making funds available for community projects, the

IFI generally provide funds as seed capital or for "pump priming"; applicants must provide other committed funding from private and/or government sources. In this way, the IFI leverages its impact while assuring that project proponents have "skin in the game" and a motivation to succeed on their own. There simply is no other institution like it, public or private.

Several projects are illustrative of the broad and varied work of the Fund:

The Townsend Business Enterprise Centre is an incubator for small businesses and entrepreneurs located on the peace line in West Belfast. A modern, multistory building, it provides free and subsidized rent for start-ups together with access to marketing, accounting, and other business advice. It is virtually full at all times and turns over to new entrants as successful businesses move on. Similar business centers are in East Belfast (referenced earlier) and Derry.

Under Wider Horizons, the Fund worked with Congressman Peter Walsh of New York to provide selection, training, travel, and housing funding for young men and women to come to the United States on specially designed work visas ("Walsh visas") to learn skills in industries useful in Northern Ireland, like tourism. An early participant we recruited to this program was the internationally famous Broadmoor Hotel and Resort in Colorado Springs, Colorado.

The Springvale Educational Village and Community Centre (discussed in more detail later) was first underwritten by an IFI commitment to locate this new and novel facility on a derelict industrial site straddling the two communities in West Belfast. Springvale was envisioned to provide technical and college offerings through the University of Ulster.

ASPIRE, discussed later, the first micro-enterprise loan fund in Western Europe, was developed through the Fund, assisted by the Northern Ireland Office (NIO) and the banks of Northern Ireland.

The work of the IFI is constant and demanding. Visiting and analyzing prospective projects, working with proponents, reassuring donors, and launching new projects takes nearly the full time and energy of the board and its staff. Board members included Lyla Steele, owner and operator of the largest commercial duck farm in Europe in County Monaghan; Caitrona Murphy, a senior executive at one of Dublin's major banks; Eamon Hanna, a CPA in Belfast; and Carmel Lynch, the owner of a small business from County Cavan. Each of them spent countless hours on the road, crisscrossing the province and the border regions to promote the work of the Fund. Pat Kenny, the managing partner of Deloitte in Dublin, also brought his considerable financial expertise and seasoned political judgment to the Fund board. My fellow Observers all played important roles:

Carlo Trojan, from the European Union, brought a deep and broad perspective from the Continent and his own deep background in the Brussels government. Speaking five languages fluently, he made good on the EU's commitment to match our US contribution, even though the EU was already providing substantial redevelopment and structural funds to Ireland. Carlo went on to serve as secretary general of the European Commission.

Bob Halverson, a large, engaging man whom no one would ever mistake for anything but an Aussie, was the Australian high commissioner (ambassador to the UK from a Commonwealth country) who had served as speaker of the lower house of the Australian parliament. Quick to a loud laugh and warm to everyone, he was keenly aware of the importance of our work and its meaning to the descendants of Ireland who had helped found his nation.

Eddie Stephens, a compact and energetic career diplomat, was New Zealand's high commissioner to London, whose duties also included the IFI. He, too, knew full well the significance of the Fund and its importance to Kiwis of Irish descent.

And last, but by no means least, Ted McConnell. Ted was Belfast born, a Catholic product of Queens University and its law school at a time when Catholics were a small and obvious minority at Queens. Finding career opportunity more than difficult in Northern Ireland, he had immigrated to Canada with his lovely bride, Pauline, the daughter of an assassinated Catholic RUC policeman. Ted had made his way and his fortune in finance and money management in Toronto and had been appointed by succeeding Canadian administrations, liberal and conservative, to serve as Canada's observer to the IFI. Charming beyond even Irish standards, Ted was a sharp business mind who carefully reviewed financial statements and business proposals. He became my good friend and mentor who took me under his wing and no doubt saved me from more than one self-embarrassment on the board.

From flagship projects like Springvale (described in Chapter 10) to small economic initiatives in remote fishing villages on the Antrim Coast, Willie and the IFI have established themselves as the vital economic regeneration institution in Northern Ireland and the border counties of the Republic of Ireland. President Clinton repeatedly recognized and praised the work of the IFI and made it the centerpiece of US policy and economic aid to the north of Ireland. As he said to the White House Trade and Investment Conference for Ireland in 1995:

> Ours is the first administration ever to include appropriations for the International Fund for Ireland. The IFI has lived up to our hopes for it. The Fund supports over 3,000 economic development projects, and has created some 22,000 jobs in areas that were recruiting grounds for paramilitaries. It is promoting cooperation across the border and between communities. The record challenges us to go even further. So we have increased our funding request for IFI to $60 million over the next two years.

Remarks by President Clinton, White House Trade & Investment Conference for Ireland (source: Archives of William Jefferson Clinton, Clinton Library, Little Rock, Arkansas).

Over the eight years of the Clinton administration, the United States contributed more than $100 million to the IFI, more than all other US administrations combined from Reagan to Obama.

My work with the IFI took me all over the north of Ireland for eight years; indeed, no one from the Clinton administration spent more time on economic initiatives on the ground in the province and the border regions.

From Donegal to County Down, from the Antrim coast to Armagh, from Downpatrick to Derry, and from Omagh and Enniskillen to Belfast, I logged countless miles, visiting innumerable IFI projects and working with Fund applicants and recipients. I shared the insightful company of my fellow observers and board members—men and women who live and work in this land and have personally committed themselves, their time, and their expertise to peace and prosperity. And never did I hear a sectarian word or witness a sectarian decision at the IFI. Willie and the IFI board had simply set a tone and agenda that was well beyond it.

In early 2001, it was time for me to leave the IFI. After eight years as US Observer, four as Special Advisor to the President, and more than fifty transatlantic journeys, it was time, as I told the *Irish Times*, for "new legs" under a new administration. But as Willie has said so often, "one never leaves the Fund"—and I haven't. I stay in touch with Willie and others, such as Dermot Gallagher, Pat Kenny, and Ted McConnell. As a token of appreciation for my service, the IFI board gave me a traditional (and working) wooden spinning wheel, a symbol of Northern Ireland's past and, I firmly believe, its entrepreneurial and self-reliant future. I treasure it as a proud trophy and powerful symbol.

Traveling during the Presidential transition, December 1992; inscription: "To Jim --
once more giving me wise counsel."

The author and President Clinton, conferring after a run

Instructions from POTUS, Belfast airport tarmac, 1995

The author, briefing the White House Press Corps on post-Good Friday Agreement developments

Father Myles Kavanagh and Sister Mary Turley with Jim Lyons, Presidential visit, Odyssey Hall, Belfast, December, 2000

Senator Daniel Patrick Moynihan, Prime Minister Tony Blair, Jonathan Powell (Prime Minister Blair's Chief of Staff), James M. Lyons, and Senator Ted Kennedy on the right (U.S./British Bilateral Conference on Northern Ireland, 1997)

Oval Office, St. Patrick's Day 1999: Left to right: Jim Lyons, Jim Steinberg, Deputy Nat'l Security Advisor; Larry Butler, NSC Staff member; Ambassador Mike Sullivan; National Security Advisor Sandy Berger, the President, and Secretary of State Madeleine Albright.

With the DUP leadership at Stormont: the author, Peter Robinson, First Minister, Sammy Douglas, and Sir Reg Empey, Chairman, UUP

The author with Geraldine McAteer at the Peace Line, Upper Springfield Road, West Belfast

The author with Geraldine McAteer (left) at the Upper Springfield Partnership Office with Bruce Finley (right), reporter for *The Denver Post*

Professor Wallace Ewert and Jim Lyons, Springvale Project under construction

David Irvine, PUP, Jim Lyons, and Gerry Adams, Sinn Fein

Billy Hutchinson, leader of the Progressive Unionist Party

Margaret McKinney and Jim Lyons, Presidential
visit, Odyssey Hall, Belfast, December, 2000

Looking down from the west wall of the Derry battlements into the Bogside, the location from which the British paratroopers opened fire on Bloody Sunday--White memorial in center

Sidebar with Willie McCarter

The IFI Observers, left to right: Carlo Trojan, European Union; Eddie Stephens, New Zealand; Ted McConnell, Canada; and Jim Lyons, USA

The IFI Observers and Chairman Willie McCarter presenting the IFI Annual Report to Taioseach Bertie Ahern, 1996

The IFI Board and Observers with First Lady Hillary Clinton

ASPIRE launch, left to right: Sir George Quigley, Jim Lyons, Northern Ireland Secretary of State Mo Mowlam, Willie McCarter, and Geraldine McAteer

Conference with POTUS in Limerick, December, 2000

J.D.'s Brunch Box, an early ASPIRE client

Katharine Koch and Jim Lyons, City Square, Belfast (in front of tank on display)

Left to right: Geraldine McAteer, Jim Lyons, Marcia Lyons, Jackie Redpath, Falls Road, Belfast (2012)

Inch Island from Rathmullan

Flight of the Earls, Rathmullan Strand, on Lough Swilly

Rathmullan House

Back row (standing): Marcia Lyons, Willie McCarter, Mary McCarter, Dermot Gallagher, and Phil Ryan; front row (seated): Maeve Gallagher, Pat Hume, John Hume, and Jim Lyons, Rathmullan House, 2012

Left to right: Maeve Gallagher, Dermot Gallagher, Marcia Lyons, Rathmullan, 2012

Phil Ryan and Marcia Lyons at the Ryan home overlooking Lough Swilly

Chapter Eight

The Border Region

In the partition of Ireland in 1922, the border between the then-free state of Ireland and the to-be-formed province of Northern Ireland was drawn to ensure a Protestant majority in the province. Originally, it was thought that all of traditional Ulster (nine counties) could be severed, but on closer inspection it was determined that this would still leave a Catholic majority. So the border was drawn accordingly, and Ulster was partitioned, too. The result was six counties in Northern Ireland (Armagh, Antrim, Derry or Londonderry, Down, Tyrone, and Fermanagh) and the twenty-six counties of what is now the Republic of Ireland. Under the Anglo-Irish Agreement, the remit of the IFI included the six counties of Northern Ireland but also the six bordering counties of the Republic of Ireland (Donegal, Leitrim, Louth, Cavan, Monaghan, and Sligo). Thus, our economic development and peace strategy included this border region of some five hundred thousand people in largely rural and agricultural areas. And here are to be encountered some very special people.

The Shannon-Erne Waterway: Dermot Gallagher

In his mid-fifties, Dermot Gallagher was the senior member of the Irish diplomatic corps and hails from the remote and rural border county of Leitrim in the Republic of Ireland. Of medium build, he is engaging, razor sharp, politically astute, and dedicated to his country, in whose foreign service he has spent his career. A graduate of University College Dublin, he has risen to be the secretary of the Department of Foreign Affairs, the top job in the ministry, having completed his service as secretary to the

Taoiseach (chief of staff to Irish Prime Minister Bertie Ahern) and Irish ambassador to the United States. During the talks that led to the Good Friday Agreement, Dermot and his colleagues Sean O'Huiginn (former Irish ambassador to the United States) and Michael Collins (later Irish ambassador to the United States) were the key players from the Irish Department of Foreign Affairs.

I first met Dermot in 1993 after I was appointed US observer to the IFI. He was then serving in Washington as Irish ambassador to the United States. Warm and politically gifted in an Irish foreign service noted for such talent, Gallagher was determined to know the "Irish players" in the new administration, such as Kevin O'Keefe, Jack Quinn (then counsel to Vice President Gore and later counsel to the President), and me. Of course, he was keen to know and understand the President himself.

Dermot and his equally talented wife, Maeve, opened both their ambassadorial residence and hospitality to us, and over the years we all became fast friends. As a former joint director of the IFI, Dermot was also a valuable resource in the ways of the Fund and its place in peace and reconciliation through economic initiatives in the North. He was of great assistance in promoting the fund to a new administration and the Congress that controlled its funding.

Among its various programs, the IFI traditionally identified one or two flagships or major projects of size and impact that promoted economic development and cross-community or cross-border reconciliation on a large scale. One such flagship is the Springvale Campus of the University of Ulster, discussed in Chapter 10. But the first flagship was the Shannon-Erne Waterway begun in the late 1980s and opened in 1993.

A longtime dream of Dermot and a few other visionaries on both sides of the border, the waterway was designed to refurbish and restore the historic nineteenth-century canals that had once joined the two major rivers on the island, the Erne in the north and the Shannon in the south. These canals and rivers had formed the commercial link that was Ireland's economic spine until the coming of the railroads made them obsolete. Few saw the potential of the canals, abandoned and overgrown, as a twentieth-century attraction for tourists, boaters, fishermen, and wildlife lovers that would bring much-needed revenues to the quaint and often isolated villages along the most pristine such waterway in Europe. But Dermot did.

After years of careful analysis and study, both governments agreed to undertake the project with the financial support of the EU Structural Fund and the IFI. After more than three years and some £35 million, the waterway became a reality in the summer of 1993. From Belfast Lough in the north, down the Erne, through the bucolic lake country, and on to the Shannon, the waterway provides an uninterrupted link from the Irish Sea to the Atlantic Ocean on the west coast of Ireland. Using a system of computerized locks, travelers on spacious and fully equipped self-piloted cabin cruisers can self-guide themselves through some of the most beautiful and unspoiled countryside in Europe while stopping to enjoy the beauty, wildlife, and charms of small Irish villages all along the way.

Since its opening, the waterway's use has steadily risen. Today, reservations for the summer must be made a year in advance, and the economic benefits to the adjacent towns and villages are readily apparent. And the vision of one dedicated Irish civil servant to economic development and cross-border cooperation is a permanent reality. To me, it is the "Dermot Gallagher Waterway" and sets a high standard as well as a model for flagship projects for years to come.

Omagh: The Bombing, Presidential Visit, Reconstruction

Omagh is located in the productive farm country of the border county of Tyrone, about an hour and a half's drive south from Derry. Its name derives from the Irish for "virgin plain." It sits between two rivers and dates from the eighth century. Chartered as a town in the seventeenth century, it was burned by supporters of Protestant King William of Orange in the same year that he defeated the Catholic King James at the Battle of the Boyne. Rebuilt along railroad links, it has become a prosperous market community for the surrounding agricultural region. Like much of rural Northern Ireland, it is a mixed community where Catholics and Protestants have learned to coexist and largely get along. It is for this reason Omagh was targeted for terrorism from a renegade IRA breakaway group. In the summer of 1998, Omagh tragically became the newest horror in Northern Ireland's bloody history.

The Good Friday Agreement had been reached in April of 1998. According to its terms, confirming votes needed to be conducted in both the Republic of Ireland and Northern Ireland. This referendum was held later that spring; the agreement was overwhelmingly ratified in the Republic of Ireland and received the needed majority of votes in Northern Ireland. A new and proportional government was in formation, and the promise of political and social stability seemed at hand.

However, on a warm and sunny Saturday morning in August, when the town market would be filled with weekly shoppers from the outlying areas, a republican splinter group (most likely the so-called real IRA) deployed and detonated the worst bombing attack on a civilian population in the history of the Troubles. Twenty-nine people—children, men, and women (including one young woman pregnant with twins)—were blown apart, some literally vaporized. Hundreds more were injured, some for life. Adding to the vicious nature of the attack, the customary "IRA warning" was either garbled or was deliberately misdirected so that people rushed from the safe end of town to the other end, where the bomb was hidden in a car. The number of dead and wounded was thus multiplied several fold.

We, like the rest of the world, were shocked and stunned. Five months after the Good Friday agreement, and two months after the all-island referendum that overwhelmingly ratified it, it had seemed that Northern Ireland was on the verge of lasting peace. President Clinton had already planned and announced a trip to Ireland, north and south, just weeks earlier. Now everything seemed shattered, just like Main Street in Omagh. Internally at the White House, some thought the Clinton trip should be canceled; others thought the trip should go forward, but then, what to do about Omagh? I was in the camp that argued for the trip and that the President could not go to Ireland and not go to Omagh. This was the President's view, and he made it known that he wanted to meet privately with the victims and their families if the Blair government approved. It did, and the prime minister and Cherie Blair agreed to accompany the Clintons to Omagh.

Out of respect for the privacy and pain of the victims and their families, the President and Prime Minister decided not to take the usual entourage but only their wives and a few senior staff, including Senator George Mitchell and me. The other members of the presidential delegation—businessmen and businesswomen, senators, and congressmen—were to go on to Armagh, where a major rally would take place later. We would join them for the rally, but first we went to Omagh.

We met with the victims and their families—several hundred people—in a small community center outside of town. The event was closed to the public and press—just the President and First Lady, the Blairs, and a few of us, including George Mitchell and me. Crowds lined the roads from town to the center. Mostly, they stood in stunned silence as our motorcade passed. Inside the packed community center, the President started on one side of the room, the Blairs on the other. The President and First Lady did what they do so well—slowly worked from family group to family group, speaking soft words of sorrow and sympathy. Invariably, one or both of them held hands or shared a hug and some tears. I watched this repeated over and over again. And then we came to the Gallagher family.

Claire Gallagher was a pretty fifteen-year-old, a classic Irish lass—if you looked beyond the bandages covering her eyes. Two weeks earlier, she was an aspiring pianist planning to study classical music at a noted Scottish conservatory. Now, Claire was blind in both eyes and, as she said, not able to read music anymore. She stood with her shocked parents and two young girlfriends providing support on each side. The President and First Lady embraced her, her parents, and her friends, and they offered words of comfort and encouragement. Then, George Mitchell stepped quietly forward, embraced her, and softly said, "Beethoven wrote some of his best music after he lost his hearing." She nodded, and her parents smiled as best they could through their tears. And I again realized—fighting to hold back my own tears—that George Mitchell was one of the most extraordinary men of my lifetime.

Later, we toured the blasted area of Main Street in Omagh. The street was roped off, and only our small party—the Clintons, the Blairs, and a few of us staff—walked it, alone and in eerie and isolated silence. The bomb had literally devastated the lower end of Main Street and blown down walls two blocks away. Three elderly women who ran a floral shop had left the security of their shop up the street and gone to what they thought was safety. They were standing next to the car when it exploded; they were identified by dental records. Their quaint shop had become a makeshift memorial with flowers, wreaths, and cards piled high against the door. We paid our respects and quietly left for Armagh, shaken and moved.

About six months later, I returned—alone—to Omagh. The British and Irish governments, in partnership with the IFI, had dedicated emergency relief funds to help rebuild the town. Unannounced and unnoticed, I wanted to see for myself what had been and could yet be done. I walked Main Street, looked in the rebuilt shops, and stopped by the town council offices. The affected area was now being redeveloped and made even more attractive than before with a lovely river walk just behind Main Street. But the memory of that awful August morning hung heavy in my mind. Only now, in the aftermath of the Oklahoma City bombing and our own tragedy of September 11, do I have some limited understanding of Omagh and what it means to that community and Northern Ireland.

St. Patrick's Day, March 17, 1999: the White House again hosted the usual St. Patrick's Day celebration. Once again, the Clintons invited us to be their guests and to spend the night in the White House. Over the years since the first gala in 1993, the demand for invitations had outstripped the capacity of the venerable old building. Hundreds of prominent Irish Americans had received much-sought-after invitations, and the major political figures, north and south, came to Washington in what had become a major annual ritual. Large tents were erected on the south lawn, and a stage was erected for the evening's entertainment: Mary Chapin Carpenter, James Galway, and Phil Coulter.

During his wonderful performance, Phil invited a young pianist to come onto the stage and join him in a song. Claire Gallagher, guided by her parents, stepped onto the stage and, as she was recognized, brought the crowd roaring to its feet. She played Phil Coulter's piano to a spellbound crowd of hard-bitten politicians—Catholic, Protestant, and American—and all were unabashed in their emotions. Truly, I thought, this is an event of great power that cannot be lost on those who oppose peace. For, in the end, the strength and courage of people such as Claire Gallagher and her family must and will overcome.

One of my other enduring memories of these annual St. Patrick's Day White House parties involved an unexpected kindness to my parents. They had been invited to join Marcia and me in Washington for the St. Patrick's Day gala, and we made a special event of it. During the day, I took my dad to the memorial for President Roosevelt, the WW II memorial, and the newly opened memorial to Korean veterans. Dad, his own father dead, became head of the family at fifteen during the teeth of the Depression. Working his way through college and law school, he enlisted after Pearl Harbor and had served in the South Pacific and Korea. Roosevelt was one of his heroes, and my father was visibly moved by the larger than life-sized statues of the poncho-clad GIs, moving on eternal and silent patrol across a frozen Korean battlefield.

That evening, as we were preparing in our hotel for the party, the White House called me and extended the President's personal invitation for the four of us to spend the night there, my parents to be in the Lincoln bedroom. My parents were speechless. The White House sent a car for us, whisked us through the gates on the South Lawn, moved them into the residence, and made them honored guests for the night. It is a lifetime memory.

This extraordinary kindness and thoughtfulness was and is characteristic of Bill Clinton, whose respect for the older generation of Americans is deep and abiding. It was also yet another example of his warmth and generosity to me and my family.

Crossmaglen and John O'Fee

Crossmaglen is a small, picturesque town in south Armagh County. Quaint cottages and shops surround a small village green. It is located about two kilometers inside Northern Ireland, and it shouldn't be: Crossmaglen is more than 90 percent Catholic and nationalist. But for some bureaucrat's haste in drawing the border eighty years ago, the town would be where it belongs—in the Republic of Ireland.

South Armagh was known to the British Army as "bandit country," for it is here that the notorious South Armagh Brigade of the IRA had for years harassed, attacked across the border, and hidden from the British Army.

The British have responded with helicopter surveillance, day and night, and constant patrols by soldiers and the SAS, the elite British paratroopers or "paras." They have also built a large, squat concrete blockhouse/barracks in the center of Crossmaglen's town square. With thick walls thirty feet high topped by concertina wire, large searchlights, and the regular comings and goings of noisy armed helicopters, the blockhouse is a constant and provocative statement from the British army to the people of this community.

Another perspective of Crossmaglen was provided in a front-page article by Bruce Finley, international reporter for the *Denver Post*, who in 2000 visited Northern Ireland with me:

> Crossmaglen, Northern Ireland: Head south from Belfast to the embattled green pastures and villages of County Armagh, and see what Denver lawyer Jim Lyons is up against as he tries to secure peace.
>
> Five British soldiers crouching in full combat camouflage, lugging machine guns, creep through the Crossmaglen market square. Townspeople look away, shopping for fish, flowers, newspapers, pushing children in strollers.
>
> Military helicopters clack overhead. A fortified brown tower, surveillance cameras swiveling on top, looms over the square. One soldier listens through an earpiece. "It's a normal patrol," he says on this recent spring morning, like what police would do in any town, any city in the world.
>
> Angry farmers just off the square in Paddy Short's pub complain about the helicopters landing in their pastures. "The war won't end," 81-year-old pub keeper Short declares, "until the British soldiers leave."

The Denver Post, April 23, 2000.

The fortified tower and block house are also an irresistible target for the IRA. Snipers and mortars have been aimed at the structure, often endangering the local community. Against such danger a remarkably brave young man named John O'Fee spoke out.

John is the son of a local doctor and the nephew of the late Cardinal O'Faigh (O'Fee). He is small and slight, in his late thirties, and politically active in the moderate nationalist party, the SDLP. His political mentor is Seamus Mallon, the white-haired professor/orator from Newry turned political leader and the first deputy first minister in Stormont. John is well respected in Armagh and represents a moderate nationalist view that abhors violence. Consistent with these beliefs, he spoke out against IRA attacks on the blockhouse that endangered the innocent community. For this, he paid a terrible price.

One night in 1994, returning to his parents' isolated home outside town, John was attacked and savagely beaten by IRA thugs. Left bleeding, with several limbs broken, and near death on the driveway, he was discovered by his mother, who staunched his blood with her own hands and screamed for the help that came and saved his life. After an extensive convalescence, he returned to work and politics, eventually being elected to Stormont's Local Assembly after the Good Friday Agreement.

I first met John in 1995 on an IFI visit to Crossmaglen, where we had funded a community center. After touring the center and walking around the town under the watchful eyes in the helicopters and blockhouse, we went to his parents' home for "tea and a chat." Chain smoking and with visible scars on his face and hands, John spoke quietly but urgently about the need for political structures to replace the violence practiced by both sides. Under the attentive and worried gaze of his mother, John was undaunted in his resolve to speak out and move forward from the sectarian abyss.

And indeed he has done just that. Now, several years later, John is a respected member of his party and the assembly. He represents his South Armagh constituency with skill and dedication. I have seen him from time to time in Belfast or at Stormont. He is quick to smile but still chain smokes and tries hard to cover his slightly shaking hands. And he still carries the scars, inside and out, that will forever mark him and Crossmaglen in my memory.

Chapter Nine

ASPIRE

This part of the story deals with the conception, development, and birth of the first micro-enterprise loan fund in Western Europe—ASPIRE. It is also the story of the men and women who brought the idea to fruition in Belfast and a very special man, Sir George Quigley.

Background

Micro-enterprise lending had its origination in rural Bangladesh in the 1970s. Mohammed Yunus conceived the notion that by pooling their few rupees, impoverished women could support each other in purchasing the necessary raw materials and crude looms necessary to make and sell cloth and garments in local marketplaces. Funds were loaned, subject to market interest, and guaranteed by the group. As loans were repaid, additional funds were available for new borrowings. Eventually, the fund grew into a bank, Grameen Bank, that became a model throughout the world, and Yunus went on to be a Nobel laureate.

In the United States, the idea was adapted and applied to chronically disadvantaged rural and some urban areas as a means of creating entry-level capital and developing entrepreneurship. A few governments—local and state—underwrote initial but isolated efforts. In Arkansas, a progressive young governor named Bill Clinton embraced the concept during the 1980s.

In Illinois, the owners of a commercial bank in a deteriorating and changing neighborhood of Chicago took the idea one step farther.

Combining the features of a micro loan fund with advisory services to first-time entrepreneurs and "micro" businesses, South Shore Bank developed a new type of commercial bank that was a capital source and support system for bringing budding black entrepreneurs into the mainstream local economy of Chicago.

I had seen the success of the South Shore Bank during my community banking years in Chicago and had followed it with interest. I also knew from Governor Clinton of his pilot state agency in Arkansas that had operated in a similar fashion. By 1997, it seemed to me that this was an idea whose time had come for Northern Ireland, and I decided to propose it to the White House and the IFI. Approval to develop a proposal was quickly given.

My first step was to try to obtain the support, financial and otherwise, of the notoriously conservative banking community in Northern Ireland. And that meant starting with the dean of the banking community, Sir George Quigley, the chairman of Northern Ireland's leading bank, Ulster Bank.

Sir George

Sir George Quigley is tall, slender, and gracefully patrician. He is a PhD and gifted with broad intelligence and wide-ranging intellectual interests (including a surprising expertise in the American Civil War). He has keen political judgment and Churchillian language skills, both spoken and written. He, in fact, could be the quintessential British gentleman in a Noel Coward play. But this impression is not the complete measure of the man. To understand Sir George Quigley, a bit of Irish history is required.

As discussed earlier, in the seventeenth century, the Tudors defeated the earls of Donegal and Ulster, the last of the Gaelic chieftains who fled to Europe, abandoning their lands and property, in the Flight of the Earls. England systematically directed the repopulation of their former strongholds by giving land to Scots and British immigrants loyal to the Crown. Known as the Ulster Plantation, it resulted in an Anglo-Irish aristocracy in Ulster and elsewhere in Ireland. Its descendants controlled the land, industry, and politics of the region for the next three hundred fifty years. Into this Anglo-Irish ruling class was born George Quigley in Moneymore, County Londonderry, in 1930.

Young George Quigley was educated at the then all-Protestant Queens University in Belfast and earned a PhD in medieval ecclesiastical history in 1955. Undecided about his future, he applied for and was accepted into the Northern Ireland Civil Service. Rising through the ranks, he found himself at its head at the outbreak of the Troubles and at the height of the civil rights movement in Northern Ireland.

Years of repressed frustration of the Catholic community was directed at all employers, including the civil service, who were accused of practicing systematic employment discrimination against Catholics. Inflamed by demagogues like Ian Paisley, the Protestant establishment generally reacted with angry refusal to consider reforms, which were regarded as a direct threat to their way of life. But not George Quigley.

Despite his roots and background, Quigley worked steadily and diligently to create equality and opportunity within the civil service. Not only did he recruit Catholics, he saw that deserving Catholics were promoted and evaluated in their careers based on merit, not religion. For this, George was branded a sellout, was often socially shunned, and even had his life threatened by so-called loyalist paramilitaries. But he persevered and succeeded in truly opening the civil service to the Catholic community for the first time in its history.

Throughout this difficult period, George was sustained and supported by his partner and wife, Moyra. A slight and intense woman of great erudition, she is one of the first (and very few) women to graduate from law school at Queens. Moyra had met George while working in the Ministry of Commerce. Although she was a lawyer, there were few if any jobs for females in the profession. They fell in love; after their marriage and in accordance with the prevailing norm, Moyra left the civil service and her promising career. She did not, however, leave behind her passion for charity and her special interest in preserving the art, architecture, and cultural institutions of Belfast, to which she has devoted herself ever since. She has been and remains today a stalwart in her community and champion of these causes.

Upon his retirement from the civil service, George was recognized with a knighthood. Eschewing a comfortable retirement, Sir George embarked on a new career as chairman of the venerable Ulster Bank and quickly became one of the pillars of the business community. It was to him I went in late 1997 with my micro-enterprise loan concept.

From Concept to Reality

Sir George immediately recognized the value of a micro loan fund and its potential benefits for Northern Ireland. He recalled that Jonathan Swift, while Dean of St. Patrick's Church in Dublin and before he wrote *Gulliver's Travels*, had established a similar fund out of his own pocket for tradesmen to buy tools and materials. But skilled politician that he is, Sir George urged patience and the cultivation of the necessary constituencies: the banking community, of course, but also community leaders, government agencies charged with business development, and key political leaders. To achieve this, we agreed on a workshop-style conference to which these important constituents would be invited. This was held in late February 1998 at the Wellington Park Hotel in Belfast. Sir George agreed to serve as chairman and the keynote speaker.

The daily planning and political spadework for this conference was largely in the hands of my State Department assistant (and later deputy), Katharine Koch. Petite, multitalented, and highly charged, Katharine, a veteran Foreign Service officer, had been selected by me from a small group of candidates for a position as my assistant within the State Department. Her selection proved to be a lucky masterstroke on my part and a key to our later mission successes.

In the fall of 1997, the President appointed me to succeed Senator Mitchell as Special Advisor to the President and Secretary of State for economic initiatives in Northern Ireland and the border counties of the Republic of Ireland. Senator Mitchell and the White House had determined that he should concentrate on his role as facilitator and chairman of the peace talks and that the economic initiative portfolio should be reassigned. Despite some maneuvering by other agencies of the government, the portfolio needed to be under the aegis of the White House and the President to underscore its importance and the President's personal commitment. Given my experience at the IFI, its importance to the Clinton administration's work in Northern Ireland, and my relationship with the President, I was the logical choice.

As a result, I became an official employee of the State Department (although I waived any salary). I had been assigned a neat but comfortable office suite on the third floor of the State Department, complete with a private office, small conference room, a secure communications system and safe for classified materials, a secretary, and Katharine. ASPIRE was our first major project together.

Katharine immediately became immersed in our work and in meeting the key players in Northern Ireland. Critically important, she helped me avoid the bureaucratic shoals and labyrinths of the State Department while we tried to develop close working relationships with the other US governmental agencies whose activities in Northern Ireland we were charged with coordinating. These included the Small Business Administration and the Departments of Agriculture, Labor, and Commerce, each of which was operating assistance programs or memoranda of understandings (MOUs) in Ireland. She was simply ideal for what we had to do and quickly made herself invaluable.

Of course, I had underestimated the task. This concept seemed so obviously suitable that I could not envision any opposition in Northern Ireland or within the US government. Wrong, on both counts. In Northern Ireland, there was concern such a program duplicated existing government programs, that a loan rather than grant approach would not be well received in the communities, and that funds could not be found. In the US government, certain members of the International Trade Agency (ITA) of the Commerce Department—regarding themselves in competition with me and the State Department—openly attacked the concept and worked behind the scenes to derail it. So we set about a campaign to win support in Northern Ireland. As for the ITA dissidents in the Commerce Department, I simply ignored them and set about bringing my friend (and Secretary of Commerce) Bill Daley on board with the idea. A former Chicago banker who was well familiar with South Shore Bank, he could not have been more supportive, and the backbiting from ITA diminished considerably.

The March roundtable/workshop was a success and resulted in a commitment to undertake a feasibility study and business plan. For this we commissioned Colin Stutt, a well-regarded economic consultant in Northern Ireland, and Janney Carpenter of Shorebank Advisory Services in Chicago. Working together and funded with a pilot grant from the IFI, they produced a positive need and market assessment and the first concrete expression of our concept in late summer 1998. We did, however, need to change the name. Our working title was Entrepreneurial Growth Trust or EGT. It was pointed out that the acronym sounded like "eee-ghit" or "idiot" in an Irish accent. Katharine contemplated the problem and came up with a most fitting name, ASPIRE.

Political support was also needed. Secretary of State Mo Mowlam—as she did so often on our projects—played a key role in this effort and put her considerable personality and energy fully behind us. Speaking for the British government and Prime Minister Blair, she publicly endorsed the project and pledged her assistance. She worked skillfully with Gerry Loughran, then permanent secretary of the Department of Development, Enterprise, and Trade (DETI); the two of them circumnavigated the skeptical Northern Ireland bureaucrats and found funding. It was for me then to raise the balance of the targeted funds (£1 million) from the banks and other sources.

From the beginning, it was our vision that the funding needed to have a significant private-sector source and character. Otherwise, this would be regarded as just another government grant program, and it was essential that the fund not be that if it was to succeed in the long run. Money lent had to be repaid and at interest rates reflecting market risk if good business practices were to be developed by the borrowers. We thus set out to secure two-thirds of the funds from the banks and the IFI as seed capital.

The IFI board reviewed our proposal at a meeting in Sligo. Caitriona Murphy, the assigned board member and an executive with Allied Irish Bank, closely studied the projections and business plan and pronounced herself satisfied with a few modifications. The IFI board—with me excusing myself from its deliberations even though I had no formal vote—unanimously approved. That left the openly resistant banks.

The Northern Ireland banks are not dissimilar to banks everywhere—cautious, tedious, and inclined to say no. Here, they banded together behind their association, to whom they sent our proposal "for study." I knew, and Sir George knew, this could be its graveyard. But nevertheless, he once again urged me to be patient and let the process (and him) work. He then set about the task in his own inimitable fashion.

Months passed with no word from the banks. Although I was busy with other projects, I was becoming increasingly frustrated and increasingly pessimistic about whether the banks would come to the table. But I had underestimated Sir George. Using his considerable charm and stature, he had persuaded his own board at Ulster Bank to support the project and then persuaded Gerry McGinn, the young, rising star and president of the Bank of Ireland, to do the same. With those two committed, the other two banks and the association followed suit, and we finally had our funding package completed.

Formation and Opening

We now needed a corporate structure to receive the funds and operate the institution and loan portfolio. We also needed competent management and a board of directors. Once again, Katharine Koch played a key role. Interviewing countless candidates for the executive management position, she found Niamh Goggin, a woman with commercial lending experience and a strong familiarity with personal credit operations in Belfast neighborhoods. She was ideal. We also formed a board of established financial professionals and community leaders like Jackie Redpath and Geraldine McAteer, who, despite their overextended commitments, agreed to make time for this groundbreaking project. Unfortunately, Sir George, by then serving as chair of the critical Parades Commission, was simply unable to find the time to serve as our first chairman, but he remained our guiding light.

Our grand opening was at the newly renovated Edge Centre in Laganside in September 1999. Mo Mowlam, Gerry Loughran, Willie McCarter representing the IFI, and representatives of each of the banks were present at the well-attended reception and press conference. Sir George gave the keynote address, again noting the earlier work of Jonathan Swift.

Like ASPIRE, Dean Swift also insisted that the loans be interest-bearing and be repaid. Sir George also said this:

> All of us often talk about the need for enterprise in business. But nowhere is enterprise more needed than in the field of public policy. The team which created ASPIRE can truly be termed policy entrepreneurs. We need far more policy entrepreneurs throughout the whole area of public affairs.
>
> We talk, too, about the crucial importance of networks and partnerships. ASPIRE shows what can be done when all the players are tuned together to achieve maximum performance.
>
> And ASPIRE illustrates the need for the animator, who kick starts it and keeps the revs up. I have never seen in action a more effective animator than Jim Lyons, most ably aided and abetted by the charming but redoubtable Katharine Koch. The Secretary of State [Mo Mowlam] has taken a keen interest throughout and has been a constant source of encouragement.
>
> They say that, to create real change, you have to be able to *envision* the new future. I remember somebody saying about Texans (who we know do things big) that they create a fantasy and make it a reality. Jim Lyons, being from Colorado, is much more understated but he can dream and he can make it come true. We have a tremendous memory bank in Northern Ireland. Would that we could swap it for a bank of dreams.

Remarks of Sir George Quigley, ASPIRE opening, September 1999.

Since its opening and to date, ASPIRE has made scores of loans, no one larger than several thousand pounds. Its repayment history is an outstanding 95 percent or higher. It has fulfilled its vision and is creating new small businesses and local jobs in the most disadvantaged neighborhoods, Catholic and Protestant. Funds were lent (and repaid) by a wide variety of small-business owners, including a hairdresser who expanded her shop with additional sinks, an auto mechanic whose new tools let him leave the dole, a printer who bought more equipment for her growing business, and a florist who was able to expand her business with deliveries from a newly acquired used lorry.

When our administration ended in early 2001, ASPIRE was up, running, and thriving. Unfortunately, without any support and oversight from the new administration, the banks began to back away and eventually withdrew their financial support. The micro loan portfolio was picked up by a government agency and continues to offer micro loans. But the future we saw for ASPIRE—for Belfast, Derry, and beyond—was not realized. Nevertheless, its promise still remains.

Chapter Ten

Springvale

Springvale is a derelict industrial site off the Springvale Road in upper West Belfast. A steep and ugly slash of ground, littered with broken concrete and debris, it sits across the road from Mackey's, the now closed textile machine manufacturing company that employed Catholics from the Falls and Protestants from the Shankill. (Mackey's was the site of President Clinton's major address in Belfast on his first visit in November 1995.) An exciting new future for Springvale was the dream of a man named Wallace Ewart.

Wallace, or Professor Ewart as he is more properly known, is a senior computer scientist at the University of Ulster. He had long dreamed of a campus of the university to be located in the heart of West Belfast, where higher educational facilities are nonexistent, far from the green lawns and tree-lined campuses of Queens or the University of Ulster in suburban Jordanstown. He envisioned an "educational village," a campus that would provide a nonsectarian resource center and offer traditional and vocational education to both communities in a central location between the Falls and the Shankill. The concept was to attract students—including adults—for technical and vocational training, much like community and junior colleges in the United States. Eventually, access to a four-year institution, the University of Ulster, would become available. Springvale was ideal—all he needed was about £80 million and the commitment of the university, the Northern Ireland Office, and the British government.

The idea had been floated to a number of organizations, including the IFI, which had been asked to consider this proposal as a flagship or major, multiyear project. It caught my attention, and I determined to learn all that I could. After examining the staff work of the IFI and numerous meetings with the education ministry, local community leaders, and politicians, I embraced the idea and agreed to take it forward with the IFI. But facing other pressing economic issues, the government of Prime Minister John Major and his secretary of state for Northern Ireland, Patrick Mayhew, had little appetite for pursuing such a bold and potentially controversial commitment. However, Willie McCarter and I convinced the IFI board that the idea had merit, and we determined to keep funds—£5 million—set aside until a more opportune time.

That time came in 1995, when Marjorie "Mo" Mowlam became Secretary of State for Northern Ireland—in effect, the British governor of the province. A plainspoken and sometimes delightfully profane ally of new Prime Minister Tony Blair, she had brains, wit, guts, and the political instincts and nerve of a Chicago ward boss. She and I hit it off immediately and became friends (and occasionally co-conspirators). Together, we resolved to work to see Springvale become a reality. It was to take four years and no small investment of political capital (mostly hers). First, questions were raised about the need for such an educational outlet, given the existing facilities offered elsewhere in the city. But this failed to recognize the long isolation of West Belfast from the greater community and the need for ready access to educational opportunities at "ground zero" of the Troubles. This was especially true for the loyalist community, which had long eschewed higher education when the apprentice system offered ready jobs to the sons, nephews, and cousins of those already working in the mills and shipyards.

Next, the educational institutions—Belfast Institute for Further and Higher Education (BIFHI) and the University of Ulster—engaged in a long turf war and were unable to come to an agreement as to the management and administration of Springvale or what course offerings should be made and by whom. Faculty infighting compounded the problem.

But, in the end, and after five long years, the project moved forward with the IFI seed money and some £75 million from the Blair government, BIFHI, and the University of Ulster. In September 1998 on President Clinton's second visit to Belfast, he and Tony Blair came to the site to break ground in a formal ceremony.

The day was sparkling, clear, and festive. A US congressional delegation was present, as were Education Secretary Dick Riley and Commerce Secretary Bill Daley. Mo Mowlam joined First Lady Hillary Clinton and Prime Minister Blair and his wife Cherie (also a successful lawyer). Willie McCarter, Senator Mitchell, Gerry Adams, and I sat side by side on the dais. Both the President and Prime Minister made specific mention of my work. That, and the culmination of our hard work, was especially gratifying.

After thanking those involved, including Mo, Willie, and me, the President marked the occasion with these words:

> Indeed, the future has begun. And clearly the best path to a future that involves every citizen of every circumstance in every neighborhood is a strong education. Springvale Educational Village will help you get there. It will be a living, breathing monument to the triumph of peace. It will turn barren ground into fertile fields cultivating the world's most important resource, the minds of your people, providing opportunity not just for the young but for those long denied the chance for higher learning, creating jobs in neighborhoods where too many have gone without work for too long, bringing more technology and skill so that Northern Ireland at last can reap the full benefits of this new economy, creating unity from division, transforming a barbed wire community that keeps communities apart into common ground of learning and going forward together.

Remarks of President Clinton, Springvale groundbreaking, September 1998 (source: Archives of William Jefferson Clinton, The Clinton Library, Little Rock, Arkansas).

The first phase of construction was undertaken with an imposing and handsome multipurpose community resources center and initial classroom space. Changing budgetary circumstances then required a refocus of Springvale to a more vocational educational mission. Under the leadership of Dr. Gerry McKenna, president and vice chancellor of the University of

Ulster, a new partnership was forged with the BIFHI and Northern Ireland government that was to allow the full mission and vision of Springvale to be achieved. A unique facility that would provide a cross-community magnet, employment, and local educational opportunity for hundreds if not thousands, Springvale was expected to someday compare with other such bold experiments like the Circle Campus of the University of Illinois on Chicago's west side or the Auraria campus in downtown Denver.

But it was not to be. After we left office, the educational institutional infighting intensified, pledged funds were delayed, and ultimately the University of Ulster withdrew from the project, citing financial problems. A government audit later concluded that the project lacked a clear vision, poor risk management, and a single independent body to oversee project management. The auditors also called for greater communication with the communities involved.

Today, Springvale still sits with its promise largely unrealized. But the core structures are there, waiting for the educational and governmental will to make it happen. As with much else in Northern Ireland, the impetus will need to come from the grassroots.

Chapter Eleven

The Clintons

No story of Northern Ireland during the 1990s is complete without the President and First Lady Hillary Clinton. They have each written their own book that sets out their personal perspectives. These are a few of mine.

I was often asked what prompted this President, unlike any other before him, to take such an active and personal interest in Northern Ireland. The answer is much like the man himself: part personal, part political, and part noble.

First, personal—in his own words:

> I was there when the Troubles began, you know. I was living in Oxford. It occupied the attention of the country obviously. I could see it coming, that religious differences were likely to lead to the same kinds of problems that racial differences had in my childhood. And I lived in a place with some pretty tough racial problems. And that had a lot to do with my going into public life.

BBC Interview with President Clinton, 1996.

President Clinton's early interest in Ireland also stemmed from his Irish roots. His mother, Virginia Cassidy, a strong and high-spirited woman, had Irish roots. Her ancestors worked as farmers in County Fermanagh, Northern Ireland. President Clinton was proud of his Irish ancestry and was one of many US presidents who had or claimed Irish roots, starting with Andrew Jackson, who hailed from an Ulster Scot family of immigrants. But Bill Clinton was the first and only one to pay special attention to the conflict in Northern Ireland.

Second, political: When Governor Clinton secured the Democratic presidential nomination in 1992, Irish American groups, keenly aware of Clinton's interest in Northern Ireland and his admiration for President Kennedy, sought to lobby for his support. The governor, in an effort to oust the then-popular president, George H. W. Bush, embarked on an elaborate and inclusive campaign. Seeking to touch breadbasket issues, he reached out to the middle and working classes, touring the country, participating in town meetings, and appearing on talk shows. Irish Americans hoped Clinton might respond to issues of discrimination and sectarian violence largely ignored by previous presidents. This hope, coupled with Clinton's determination to reach many ethnic groups, brought the presidential candidate to the Irish Forum in New York in the spring of 1992.

The Irish American activists at the forum immediately worked to lobby Clinton's support for two key issues. First, they wanted Clinton, if elected president, to back a US visa for Gerry Adams, the leader of Sinn Fein, the so-called political wing of the IRA. Previously denied a visa for his links to the IRA and listed by the Justice and State Departments as a member of a terrorist organization, Adams had sought the visa ostensibly to gain political funds for Sinn Fein but also with the announced intent of discussing an end to the sectarian violence.

Second, the NY activists asked Clinton if elected to appoint an American "peace envoy" to Northern Ireland. While promising to fulfill these requests immediately fueled opposition from northern unionists and infuriated the British government, Clinton hoped a promise to support Irish American appeals might ultimately encourage peaceful dialogue in Northern Ireland. He also foresaw the importance of international economic support. He realized that Northern Ireland's conflict prevented economic progress by deterring international trade and investment. With Northern Ireland's relationship to the United Kingdom, the Republic of Ireland, and the larger European Union—all substantial US trading partners—Clinton concluded that instability threatened international trade and thus created a legitimate financial reason for the United States to get involved in Northern Ireland.

Third, Governor Clinton had a noble conviction that the power and majesty of the presidency could successfully be brought to bear on seemingly intractable problems of peace and that the United States should have a morally based foreign policy focused on this objective. This same conviction was personified in his senior foreign policy appointments of Warren Christopher, Tony Lake, Jim Steinberg, Nancy Soderberg, and, later, Madeleine Albright. This was his goal not only in Northern Ireland but also in war-torn Central and Eastern Europe and the Middle East. But in Northern Ireland, he had personal history, ancestral roots, and the support of over forty million Americans who claim Irish descent, both Protestant and Catholic.

His early efforts were both economic and political, reflecting his view that economic opportunity was the handmaiden of peace. In his first budget sent to Congress in 1993, he became the first president to call for full and increased funding to the International Fund for Ireland (discussed in more detail in Chapter 7) and appointed as his US Observer someone known to have a direct and personal relationship with him. On the political front, he knew that he needed to take risks for peace and granted a US visa to Gerry Adams over the strong opposition of his own State and Justice Departments. This action was rewarded with the unilateral ceasefire of the IRA, matched by loyalist paramilitaries—a huge first step in the long road to the Good Friday Agreement five years later.

The ceasefire gave the Clinton administration the political space needed to develop a greater role in Northern Ireland. After granting Adams a second visa, Clinton continued to search for ways to advance the peace process. We began by organizing a special White House economic conference on Northern Ireland. This conference, held in May 1995, brought together for the first time business and political leaders of Ireland in a forum that would not have been possible on the island.

Three hundred businessmen met with one hundred business representatives from the Republic of Ireland and Northern Ireland for this White House–sponsored trade and investment conference. The goal of the conference was to promote peace and investment amongst political adversaries by highlighting the common desire for economic prosperity. Over formal morning presentations and breakout sessions in the afternoon, men and women from both communities had the opportunity to interact, often one on one, in ways that sectarianism back home would not have permitted.

In a speech made at the conference, Clinton explained:

> We must have the resources to foster peace and stand by those that take the hard risks for peace. We have seen time and again that our investments in peace whether in the Middle East, Southern Africa, Haiti, or Ireland have always yielded great benefits for the American people: in growing markets, greater stability, and increased security. I hope all those who want to see peace in Northern Ireland will keep that in mind. Peace has a price but it is a small price compared to the alternative and it is a price very much worth paying.

Remarks of President Clinton, White House Trade & Investment Conference, May 1995 (source: Archives of William Jefferson Clinton, The Clinton Library, Little Rock, Arkansas).

The conference reflected Clinton's foreign policy approach by combining economics with a plea for peace. At the conference, Clinton emphasized, "Of the gifts we can give to Ireland, this example of people joining together for the common good clearly is the greatest." Remarks of President Clinton, White House Trade & Investment Conference, May 1995.

The conference was such a success that the participants called for a follow-up conference, which we held in Pittsburgh the following year under the auspices of the US Commerce Department. This conference focused on business-to-business relationships and led to a number of Irish/American joint ventures and partnerships. In fact, in order to allow more time for this networking, we asked Secretary of Commerce Mickey Cantor to cut short his keynote address, which he graciously did.

Black Irish

The White House Trade and Investment Conference in 1995 and the US Department of Commerce Trade Conference in Pittsburgh were high-profile events, showcasing our strategy and efforts for economic development in support of a lasting peace. But other events and trade missions were of great importance as well. One of the first, in 1994, had been led by US Commerce Secretary Ron Brown and his assistant secretary, Chuck Meissner.

Ron Brown was a highly skilled and experienced politician who had come from Harlem to Middlebury College, to St. John's Law School, the National Urban League, and eventually to partnership at the DC lobbying and law firm powerhouse of Patton Boggs. Along the way, he had become active in the presidential campaigns of Ted Kennedy and Jesse Jackson. In 1992, he was in his early fifties and serving as chairman of the Democratic National Committee. He was at the peak of his career and his game.

I met Ron in the late eighties, once again thanks to Mike Driver, also a partner at Patton Boggs. Our paths crossed during the 1991–1992 Clinton campaign, and, after the nomination was secured by Governor Clinton in March 1992, Ron became an active and important member of the national Clinton team. After the election victory, the president-elect named Ron his commerce secretary, the first African American to hold that position.

One of Brown's overseas visits was to Ireland in December 1994, at the direction of the President. As US Observer to the IFI, I was invited to join his official party and gladly accepted. Senator Chris Dodd joined us for part of the trip, which was "advanced" by Mike Stratton, an old friend from Denver, a close friend of the President, and an experienced political operator in any country.

We visited with government officials and counterparts to the Department of Commerce in Dublin and Belfast, including the US Consulate in Belfast and the representatives of the International Trade Administration whose officers serve in embassies and consulates around the world. Chuck Meissner, Ron's assistant secretary, brought genuine and serious interest and enthusiasm for making the ITA as effective as possible in linking US businesses with opportunities in Northern Ireland as well as being a gateway to the European Union. This fit perfectly with our strategy, and we formed a strong working relationship that was to produce results.

A particularly memorable event on the trip was a speech that Secretary Brown gave to graduate business students who were largely from the nationalist community. Referring to his own background and race, he told them he knew something of discrimination and how one works to overcome it and succeed. It was a personal and powerful message that could only have been delivered by a black man like Ron, and the students gave him a standing ovation. Afterward, using an old expression for Irish of dark complexion and coloring thought to be descendants of Spanish sailors from the wrecked Armada, I gave him the honorary title of "Mr. Black Irish." He roared with laughter and later used the term himself.

Ron continued his focus on Northern Ireland, largely through Chuck and his staff. They worked closely with me to coordinate IFI projects with theirs, but there were other areas in the world that required their attention. One such area was the war-torn lands of the former Yugoslavia, including Bosnia and Croatia.

Hardly had the shooting stopped before Brown, Meissner, and their senior staff were touring the region in April 1996 to see what the United States could do to promote economic regeneration. Not to be deterred by weather, they were flying into Croatia at night during a severe thunderstorm. Apparently misjudging the runway and altitude, the pilots crashed into a mountainside and killed everyone on board.

An official funeral was held at the National Cathedral in Washington, DC, for both Ron and Chuck. The cabinet, members of the Senate and House, and senior officials from throughout the government attended, as well as those of us who had worked with them. A standing-room-only crowd overflowed out onto Wisconsin Avenue. President Clinton gave an emotional eulogy, at one point looking down to Ron's casket to gesture and say, "But for you, I wouldn't be here." He later recognized Ron posthumously with the Presidential Medal of Freedom.

Ron's contributions to Ireland were not forgotten either. Boston College established a scholarship in his name as part of their Irish Studies Program. And, in March 2011, the new US Mission to the United Nations building in New York was named in his honor and dedicated by Presidents Obama and Clinton.

I remember Ron and Chuck for the energy, enthusiasm, and resources they brought to bear in Northern Ireland at a critical time in its struggle toward peace and prosperity. Others on the ground in both communities witnessed their work and remember them well. Theirs was a short but important and lasting contribution to peace and prosperity in Northern Ireland. May they rest in well-earned peace.

Senator George Mitchell, Ireland Peace Envoy

The President's next step was to recruit in 1995 recently retired Senator George Mitchell. The President had been approached by the British and Irish governments and asked if the United States would play a mediator-like role in helping to restore political institutions and stability in Northern Ireland. Mitchell, the respected Senate majority leader from Maine who had announced his retirement in March 1994, was the ideal candidate for this key role. President Clinton had previously offered Mitchell a place on the United States Supreme Court, which he had declined. He did, however, accept this new position as the Special Advisor to the President and Secretary of State for peace and economic initiatives in Ireland. At a time when appointing a peace envoy remained controversial, Clinton hoped Mitchell could move the process forward through negotiation and economic support.

The highlight of 1995 was, of course, the President's first visit to Belfast and Derry in December. Arriving first before dawn in London, we helicoptered in Marine One and Two over a twinkling city that looked like London at night in the Disney movie *Peter Pan*. After a brief stop at the hotel to shower and change, we spent the day in a variety of meetings, culminating in the President's address to the combined Houses of Parliament in magnificent Westminster Hall. The next day, the President and those of us in his official party flew on to Belfast.

None of us traveling with him was prepared for the impact of his presence in a place long starved for respect and positive attention. From wheels-down on Air Force One in Belfast, to the motorcade to the city, to the speech and Christmas tree lighting on the steps of Belfast City Hall before an estimated crowd of over one hundred thousand from all over the province, he simply electrified the province with the promise of US support for peace and a new era.

The next day in Derry, thousands of people waited in the dark and cold in the small square and on the walls outside ancient Guild Hall, the site of many of our community events and IFI project launches in that town. Traveling by Navy Sea Stallion helicopters, which were unheated, loud, and fitted out for troops with web seats along the sides, we arrived late in the day and motored into the central city, where night had already fallen. We parked as close as we could to the small central square but had to walk the last distance down several ancient, narrow streets that could not accommodate the motorcade. A massive crowd, hanging from building and rooftops, waving American flags, thundered to life, when we turned the corner to enter the square as the floodlights came on to welcome us. The President took the stage with the First Lady and John Hume. John introduced the President to another roar from the crowd. Again, the President expressed his personal commitment to support for a peace process and economic renewal. The crowd roared again, and John Hume, already a legend in his home town, was for once outdone. It was another impressive and memorable event.

For me, this trip was the highwater mark of the first two years of service in Northern Ireland. It validated in dramatic terms what we had worked for, punctuated by personal presidential engagement and commitment to the people of Northern Ireland. But for all the momentum created on political and economic fronts, no peace emerged during his first term. Three hundred years of suspicion, discrimination, and violence were not to be so easily swept aside.

In the second Clinton term, the unfolding process eventually led to a momentous peace agreement in 1998, after years of tireless effort and patience on the part of Senator Mitchell and the personal intervention of the President. Still, Clinton's second term would see considerable setbacks before significant change developed. The bombing of the Canary Wharf in London in February 1996 appeared to mark the end of the IRA ceasefire. Hundreds of millions of pounds of damage from a 500 pound fertilizer bomb was done to this regenerating part of commercial London; it reverberated throughout Ireland and put the peace process in great jeopardy.

The violence carried into the summer when loyalist Orange Order parades provoked sectarian outbursts as they passed through Catholic communities like the Garvaghy Road in an effort to provoke and inflame the residents. All of this renewed violence threatened the slow but steady progress toward peace, but then the election of Tony Blair altered the downward spiral.

On May 1, 1997, Blair's Labour Party defeated John Major's conservative government. In a landslide victory, Blair became the new British prime minister. Blair's victory marked the end of sixteen years of conservative rule. His election and Labour's platform for Northern Ireland offered fresh hope to the province just as sectarian violence had all but ended the peace process.

From the beginning, Blair made Northern Ireland a priority, as evidenced by his cabinet appointment of a close ally, Marjorie "Mo" Mowlam, as Secretary of State for Northern Ireland. The new Prime Minister quickly developed a close relationship with both President Clinton and Senator Mitchell. Blair welcomed and encouraged continued US involvement. He asked the President to maintain pressure on Sinn Fein to find a way to come to the bargaining table while he concentrated his efforts on the unionists and loyalists.

Among them, Tony Blair, Bill Clinton, and the newly elected Irish *Taoiseach* Bertie Ahern accomplished a political transformation. All three leaders shared a similar political ideology (the so-called third way, beyond binary political ideologies) and a strong commitment to peace in Northern Ireland. They established excellent relations and worked to support each other in this endeavor. Such commitment and cooperation was unprecedented and was imperative to successful negotiations.

This new leadership rejuvenated the peace process and allowed negotiations to move forward, though very slowly and imperceptibly at first. But with George Mitchell's skill, patience, and determination, progress was being made. In Clinton's second term, Madeleine Albright replaced Warren Christopher to become the first female secretary of state. She, too, supported Clinton's involvement in Northern Ireland and continued to support the administration's commitment to peace.

After a six-week ceasefire, Sinn Fein joined the talks in August 1997. The prolonged and arduous negotiations reached a conclusion on Good Friday, April 10, 1998. The Belfast Agreement, better known as the Good Friday Agreement, provided an agreed framework for reconciliation through a power-sharing government. In May 1998, the agreement passed with 71 percent of the popular vote in Northern Ireland and 95 percent in the Republic of Ireland. In the first all-island vote in eighty years, 85 percent of those who voted approved the agreement. President Clinton, through conferences, visits, key phone calls, the appointment of George Mitchell, and courageous political risks, had played an essential role in the difficult process. More importantly, he provided optimism and reassurance when peace seemed unimaginable and illusive.

Hillary Clinton was also deeply and passionately involved in Northern Ireland. In many ways, my work there was closer to hers since we both worked primarily at the community, grassroots level. Brilliant, disciplined, and warmly compassionate, she had been keen all her career to work with and for disadvantaged people, especially women and children. As a fellow trial lawyer, I knew from our past work together that she had solid analytical abilities, great judgment, and was icy cool under fire. In short, she brought every skill to Northern Ireland that the job required. And, to boot, she was First Lady of the United States.

Hillary instinctively understood the importance of ignoring sectarianism and reaching out to both communities at the grass roots. Much of her considerable energy was invested there. Of particular importance was her Vital Voices initiative that she promoted around the world but nowhere more effectively than in Belfast. Through workshops and programs designed to identify, train, and empower women as community organizers and leaders, Vital Voices, cosponsored by Mo Mowlam in

Belfast and Derry, gave a framework to the cross-community efforts of scores of women who had endured the Troubles and worked unheralded every day for a better life for their children and families. Vital Voices, as personified by the First Lady and Mo Mowlam, legitimized these women from the neighborhoods and provided official US recognition of their extraordinary efforts. As I often said, "the women of Northern Ireland were not vital voices for peace during the Troubles; they were often the only voices." And in Hillary, these women not only found their advocate, they found their megaphone.

Led by President Clinton and First Lady Hillary Clinton, the United States paid the ultimate tribute to the debt the United States owed to the Irish by making a positive contribution to the peace process. As New York Republican Congressman Peter King once noted, while future presidents may follow Clinton's policies, none will have the same interest and intensity.

Although the Clintons' efforts in Northern Ireland did not attract the full recognition they deserved in the United States, they gained many appreciative friends across Ireland and Northern Ireland. With the same courage and determination that carried a young man from Arkansas to the steps of the White House, Clinton turned his unwavering interest and love for the people of Northern Ireland into concrete and measurable peace and social stability. As they worked to restore hope and to improve and save lives, the efforts of both Clintons showed the United States and themselves at their very best.

Chapter Twelve

Last Laps

In February 2001, I attended my last IFI Board meeting as US observer, having previously resigned in January as Special Advisor to the President. A new administration had taken office, and it was time for me to go. As I told the *Irish Times*, who had described me as the President's "eyes and ears in Northern Ireland," "new legs" were needed.

My final IFI meeting was full of nostalgia and satisfaction for eight years of effort. As with the first meeting, I brought Marcia with me to bookend this chapter in our lives. The board and observers met in Newcastle at a restored railroad and resort hotel on the coast. As usual, the board visited an IFI project, this time the newly opened St. Patrick's Centre in nearby Downpatrick, where the saint venerated by both religious traditions is said to be buried. The Centre had been under study by the IFI for several years, and funding had finally been approved in 2000. Construction was now complete, and we were given a preopening tour of the facility that included a state-of-the-art audiovisual exhibit of Patrick's life and times.

After the tour, we climbed the hill to the churchyard cemetery where Patrick's grave is marked with a large boulder bearing only the word "Patrick" in Celtic lettering. It seemed a fitting place for me to end my official work and say a short prayer to the man who had brought religious unity to Ireland so many centuries before. For as President Clinton had observed, Patrick was the only man since St. Paul to have successfully spread Christianity without a sword in his hand.

We had accepted the invitation of Martin Naughton and his gracious wife Carmen to join them at their weekend estate, Stackallen House, on our way home. Martin is one of Ireland's most successful entrepreneurs and a member of the Board of Trustees of Notre Dame University. We had come to know each other through his work on the cross-border commission created by the Good Friday Agreement, which had prominent business people from the North and the South exploring mutually beneficial economic development and common infrastructure. He was an icon on the island and put considerable time and energy into the work of the commission. He and Carmel had been among the VIPs at the President's event in Dundalk in December of the previous year.

About an hour outside of Dublin, Stackallen House is a fully restored Anglo-Irish estate from the eighteenth century. Huge, high-ceiling rooms, marble fireplaces and floors, intricate wood molding, panels, and carvings were everywhere. A collection of original Jack Yeats drawings graced the library. (Yeats had done twelve of these, each depicting a different Irish character, such as the priest, the farmer, the publican, and so on. Martin has managed to collect ten of these, one is in the Irish National Museum, and the twelfth remains lost.)

A roaring fire in the entryway greeted us and drove away the rainy chill. With lovely grounds, stables, and an imposing formal garden, it is truly a step back in time. Ambassador Mike Sullivan and his wife Jane joined us for a blustery but wonderful "weekend in the country" as the original gentry had experienced. As we left, the Naughtons gave us a signed copy of a book setting out the house's history and restoration.

Later in the early spring, now former President Clinton called to invite me to join him and his daughter Chelsea in Northern Ireland in May. He was returning to fulfill several commitments and receive an honorary degree from Queens University. I readily accepted and agreed to meet him in Derry and then travel on with him through Enniskillen and on to Belfast.

We met at the Beech Hotel outside Derry. A beautifully restored country house, the Beech served as the headquarters for the US Navy and Marines stationed in Derry during World War II. Lovely grounds and an intimate parlor (now bar) were put at our disposal. The President was accompanied by his daughter Chelsea and Jim Steinberg, who had played such a key role in Northern Ireland while serving as deputy national security advisor.

After a formal dinner in town given by the Derry community to thank him, we returned to Beech House well after midnight. After a nightcap, I headed for bed, only to be intercepted by an aide who told me the President was interested in playing cards. Given the lateness of the hour (and his professional prowess at Hearts), I said one word to the aide, "Solitaire," and went off to bed. I could hear the President's loud laughter as the aide reported my response.

The next day took us to the Ulster American Folk Park, founded by the Mellon family to commemorate their Ulster ancestry. Chelsea and I went on ahead to explore the park as anonymously as possible. A wonderful complex of thatched cottages, barns, and shops, it features a full-sized replica of the port from which the immigrants left this part of Ireland, the "coffin ships" on which they traveled, and the port of eighteenth-century Philadelphia where they disembarked. It reminds one of Williamsburg village in Virginia.

From there we went to Enniskillen, scene of a horrific bombing during the Troubles and now the location of the Clinton Peace Centre (funded in part by the IFI) that he had promised to open. A large crowd had gathered for the occasion, and several dignitaries were on hand, including Willie McCarter and Stella O'Leary, head of Irish American Democrats and a tireless advocate for Irish interests in Washington, DC. As I greeted numerous old friends, I couldn't help but remember what the town center had looked like after the devastation and senseless loss of life. This was, indeed, an important event in the continuum of the peace process and healing that must take place. It was made more special by the presence of the President.

Piling into the van for the ride to Belfast, we pulled off the main road just before the motorway at the small, quaint town of Ballygawley for an unscheduled bite of lunch. Bounding out of his car, the President simply walked into the first café he saw and then stepped back out to wave us in. In short order, we took over the small café, had some sandwiches, and posed for pictures with the locals. Coming back out to the cars, we encountered a crowd of several hundred people (likely the whole town population), whereupon the President began working the crowd and shaking hands. A nervous RUC officer asked me how long before he was likely to leave; I told him that he would not leave until he had shaken every hand in the square. And he didn't.

Arriving in Belfast, we barely had time to change and make our way to Queens for a reception and private meeting with the political leaders, including David Trimble and Gerry Adams. The Good Friday Agreement was in place but far from fully implemented. The President's encouragement and simply his presence seemed to breathe new life and purpose into those struggling to make it a complete reality.

The ceremony of investiture for the honorary degree was filled with regalia and pomp faithful to the long traditions it repeated. Senator George Mitchell, newly installed honorary chancellor of Queens, presided. But the real highlight was the President's remarks in acceptance of the honor. Abandoning his prepared remarks as he often did so well, the President set forth his vision of the world and America's role in the coming years. Full of his time-honored themes of responsibility and promise, he called for a United States working in close partnership with democracies around the world to expand political freedoms, overcome racism/tribalism, and reward those who took risks for peace. It was again a proud time to be an American and to be proud of our service in the cause of peace.

Jim Steinberg and I decided to skip the post-ceremony dinner. We both had been to enough of those over the years. We chose to spend the time over a pint or two at McGuinness Whiskey Bar, reminiscing about the last eight years. In his early forties, Jim is one of the smartest people I have ever met. Like Nancy Soderberg at the NSC, my contact there for years, he is an alumnus of Senator Kennedy's crackerjack foreign policy staff and, like Nancy, has a razor-sharp intellect coupled with sound political instincts. Both he and Nancy are not much given to self-promotion or verbosity and make delightful conversational companions with rare insights into the history they have made. They had brought much to the peace process in Northern Ireland, but we agreed that, in the end, it would be up to its people and political leaders to find their way forward to permanent stability and prosperity. Although educated as a lawyer, Jim has always preferred public policy to pleadings and interrogatories. He later went on to serve as deputy secretary of state, the number two position under Secretary of State Hillary Rodham Clinton.

My visits to Northern Ireland with the President were always long on substance and short on sleep. Traveling with the President of the United States is an honor and a challenge—just to keep up and often just to stay out of the way. Over the years, I had the privilege of traveling on Air Force One, Marine Two (the President's backup helicopter), the Navy's Sea Stallion helicopters, and various government executive jets. Hotel time was always limited, and we were always on the go with little, if any, down time.

Inside the protective bubble of a presidential delegation, one sees at close hand and has to admire the enormous staff work and preparation, the timing and choreography of movements, the White House staff (who never seems to sleep), and the constant vigilance of the Secret Service. On every occasion, I appreciated the privilege and felt the responsibility of representing my country and my President. I always tried to act as if he (and my mother) were watching.

Chapter Thirteen

Thoughts and Musings

Anyone who claims to be an expert on Northern Ireland is either ignorant or a fool. After almost ten years of on-the-ground experience, I hope I am neither. But I did learn several things about economic initiatives in support of peace, the people of Northern Ireland, and the role and responsibility of the United States.

Economic initiatives work best from the ground up and not the other way around. Community initiative, support, and commitment are essential. People must have a real stake in the outcome and be given the opportunity and responsibility to make an idea succeed. Failure is not necessarily a bad outcome if it is instructive and leads to further effort and eventual success. Examples here might include ASPIRE and Springvale, great and bold ideas whose support and time was premature.

But there is no doubt in my mind that the IFI is a model for this: seed money made available but in an accountable manner for cross-community, nonsectarian projects as determined by an independent board of local businessmen and businesswomen, not government officials or bureaucrats. The record of the IFI in this arena is unparalleled in terms of numbers of projects funded, investments leveraged, people affected, and jobs created. A joint committee of the British and Irish parliaments estimated that the IFI created over twenty-three thousand permanent jobs, funded over forty-five hundred projects, and was responsible for in excess of $1.5 billion of investment. A similar study by KPMG confirmed these results.

The IFI's performance can, however, be improved: an independent staff would help deliver more resources in less time to more worthy projects; innovation and creativity could be enhanced; and US funding needs to be secured at sustainable levels in partnership with the EU and the other donor countries. This should not be a permanent US commitment but one for the next few years until real political and economic stability exists in Northern Ireland. Unfortunately, succeeding administrations have cut IFI funding, and its operations and influence now are substantially diminished.

The moral authority and role of the United States in the world has been steadily declining in my view, and that decline has affected Northern Ireland as well. What had been a nonpartisan effort in Northern Ireland and a true foreign policy partnership between the president and a Republican-led Congress is now gone, part of the politics of polarization. In my time, Republicans like Representatives Peter King and Jim Walsh and Senator Al D'Amato were always helpful to the Northern Ireland issues, as were the Irish Democrats of the House and Senate, led by Senators Leahy, Dodd, and Kennedy. Sadly, partisan advantage—not good policy—now rules the day in Washington, and Northern Ireland (among other places) has been the loser. Perhaps the reasons for this are the obvious ones: other areas of the world (e.g., Iraq and Afghanistan) have occupied our strategic attention since September 11, 2001. New challenges for our economy have arisen since the meltdown in 2008. Health insurance, gun control, immigration reform, and other major domestic issues remain at the forefront of our national attention. And, of course, Northern Ireland is but a tiny place in the corner of Europe, and it has no oil.

Or perhaps Americans, Congress, and the White House simply believe that the job in Northern Ireland is done and requires nothing further from us. Whatever the reasons, Northern Ireland now comes up short on US priorities, much to the delight of the men of violence and political extremists on both sides of the sectarian divide. Simply put, the United States—for very little money and some modest but meaningful effort—can and should do better. The job in Northern Ireland, much like Iraq and Afghanistan, remains to secure the peace we helped broker.

But in the end, it is the people of Northern Ireland who will make the difference—as they always have. Like the men and women of Northern Ireland whose stories are part of this book, Catholic and Protestant, unionist and nationalist, the people of Northern Ireland will one day be brought together for the commonweal. The forces of economics, history, and the people will not and cannot be denied. This is the essence of the Good Friday Agreement and, indeed, the essence of democracy itself.

Along the beautiful north Antrim coast lies a spectacular and unique work of nature called the Giant's Causeway. Interlocking basalt columns in octagonal shape formed by ancient volcanoes rise in architectural symmetry from the sea and make an abbreviated bridge into the sea out toward Scotland, which is visible on the horizon. Irish myth says that the "causeway" was built by the Irish giant Finn McCool to make his way to Scotland to challenge a larger Scottish giant. Seeing he was outmatched, Finn fled back to Ireland, the Scottish giant in hot pursuit. Once back, Finn's wife disguised him as a baby. The Scottish giant, fearful of meeting Finn's presumably larger father, then fled back across the bridge, destroying it as he went. This popular and ancient myth, like so many others, has endured and swirls in the Celtic mists of this place.

However, although there was no Finn McCool, there are giants in Northern Ireland; they are no myth, nor are they afraid of large challenges. These giants are the men and women of this book and others like them who, despite the cold swells and battering of ancient sectarianism, are building a causeway to peace and a new Northern Ireland. And, unlike the Giant's Causeway, it will one day be completed.

Epilogue/Afterword

September 2012: Rathmullan and Retrospective

This book has been twelve years in the making—like fine Irish whiskey, it needed to age to reach its best. But the human memory leaks more than a barrel, and so I am sure there are significant events and individuals that I have forgotten. One such event and individual I vividly recall: I was asked to dedicate a new, IFI-sponsored community center in Castlereagh, a small community near Belfast hard hit by recession and the Troubles. One of the board members and my host was a young woman confined to a wheelchair with misshapen and deformed limbs from birth. Despite her severe handicap, her broad smile, bubbling personality, and enthusiasm for the future of her community overwhelmed me. Her name is lost to me, but her inspiration and courage is not. My apologies to her and the other special people like her throughout Northern Ireland that I met but cannot now remember.

In those twelve years, much has transpired in Northern Ireland. The major political parties were unable to hold the local assembly together, so direct rule from London was again required on several occasions. Finally, after some modifications to the Good Friday Agreement reached at St. Andrews, Scotland, the DUP, now the majority party of the unionists/loyalists, and Sinn Fein, now the majority party of the nationalists, were able to form a coalition government. This unlikely alliance has endured. Peter Robinson of the DUP is first minister and Martin McGuinness of Sinn Fein is deputy first minister. Other cabinet positions are proportionately assigned, and functioning local government is a reality.

Outbursts of sectarian violence still occur but not nearly on the frequency and scale of the Troubles. As George Mitchell recently observed, political and social stability appear to be in place in Northern Ireland. But, as President Clinton noted in 1995, quoting W. B. Yeats, "peace comes dripping slow," and much remains to be done.

In the years after my service, I traveled to Northern Ireland from time to time but not with the same frequency as before. I would visit my friends at the Department of Foreign Affairs in Dublin and take the train to Belfast to see my old acquaintances and friends and try to get out to Derry. When possible, I would take one or more of my children to see firsthand what had occupied their often absent father and give them a sense of the Irish history we helped make.

I joined the Friends of Belfast network and chaired the chapter of the Friends in Denver. We met quarterly or so to build business-to-business links between Denver, gateway to the Rocky Mountain region, and Northern Ireland. For a time, Invest Northern Ireland (INI), the economic development agency of the Northern Ireland government, maintained an office and consultant in Denver who coordinated with us and helped organize trade missions. Colorado Governor Bill Owens led just such a mission with me to Belfast, and Denver Mayor Wellington Webb did as well. (The sight of a six-foot-six African American mayor in Belfast was head-turning, to be sure.) These missions underscored the economic links between the North and the Rocky Mountain West, particularly in the areas of tourism, bioscience, and computer technology.

I have also been asked to share my experiences and lessons learned with various audiences, schools, and conferences. For example, in 2002, I was invited to participate in a weeklong conference at the International Institute for Law and Sociology housed in the magnificent medieval university in Onate, Spain. Located in the heart of Basque country about an hour from Bilbao, the IILS hosted a number of academics and conflict-resolution practitioners from around the world to present papers and discuss best practices for conflict resolution, reconciliation, and restorative justice for post-conflict societies. Northern Ireland after the Good Friday Agreement, an uncommon success story in this field of endeavor, was featured prominently.

In 1998, the political leadership, First Minister David Trimble and Deputy First Minister Seamus Mallon, toured the United States to promote the Good Friday Agreement and investment opportunities in Northern Ireland. They came to Denver, where I had promised them good things would happen. I delivered: while in Denver and in the middle of the night while staying in the Brown Palace Hotel, David learned that he and John Hume had won the Nobel Peace Prize. International press descended on Denver, and David and the prize dominated the news and elevated the coverage of the road show. We celebrated over lunch (during a heavy Rocky Mountain hailstorm), and President Clinton called with his congratulations.

In the fall of 2012, I again visited Northern Ireland after an absence of a few years. Marcia joined me, as we wanted to see old friends and see for ourselves what was new in the place. We started in Donegal, home of my ancestors, and the beautiful land around the Swilly.

We went first to Rathmullan, on the west side of the lough, where the Flight of the Earls had taken place in 1607, now marked by a modern sculpture in the small town park. Rathmullan is accessible across the lough from Buncrana by ferry (partly funded by the IFI) that operates in the summer season but is closed for the fall and winter. One thus reaches Rathmullan by driving around the lough to the west toward Letterkenny and then north to the village itself.

A short drive or walk up from the beach outside the village is the historic Rathmullan House. Built in 1820 by Anglo-Irish gentry as a large summer home, the house has now been renovated into a charming small country hotel on a hill with sweeping views of Lough Swilly and a two-mile-long strand (beach). It has charming parlors, cozy libraries, and sitting rooms heated by peat fireplaces when chill or damp is in the air. A wonderful restaurant makes this a charming hotel known throughout the province and the island.

During my time with the IFI, we had frequently conducted board meetings in similar old manors and country houses that had been converted into small hotels. Generally, we used these quaint hotels as bases for visiting Fund projects in the vicinity when we were not meeting in Belfast or Dublin. Rathmullan House had been one of these Fund venues, as had Leslie Hill in County Antrim. We had also met at Lissadell House, the Gore family estate in Sligo, near Yeats's grave with the famous and haunting epitaph: "Cast a cold eye on life, on death Horseman, pass by." (Coincidentally, this is the same Gore family whose nineteenth-century scion, Lord Gore, traveled extensively in a large and lavish hunting expedition in the Rocky Mountains and for whom the Gore mountain range near Vail, Colorado, is named. Indeed, Al Gore may be a distant relation.)

In addition to its charm and familiarity, Rathmullan House was chosen by us for its proximity to Derry, Fahan, and our friends Dermot and Maeve Gallagher, Willie and Mary McCarter, John and Pat Hume, and Reggie and Phil Ryan. We hosted a wonderful dinner for this group and enjoyed reminiscing about our work together and the bonds we had formed. Unfortunately, time, stress, and exertion has taken its toll on John Hume, and he struggled to stay in the conversation. Reggie Ryan, now suffering from advancing Alzheimer's disease, was unable to join us, but Phil came, taking a welcome break from her caregiving duties. Despite the burdens they carried, Phil and Pat Hume were as sparkling and delightful as ever.

The next day we drove to visit Reggie and Phil at their seaside dream home overlooking the Swilly. Reggie looked healthy, but his mind was not able to engage with us. We spent time with Phil; toured the beautiful house of native stone, wood, and glass; remembered great nights at St. John's Inn; walked the grounds; and took our leave with a promise to return.

We then drove on to Belfast over the Foyle Bridge with its spectacular view of Derry to the south. We were to meet the Quigleys—Sir George and Lady Moyra—for lunch at one of our favorite restaurants and one of Belfast's best, Deanes, around the corner from the Europa Hotel. As always, the Quigleys were gracious and up to date on local as well as international events, and we savored our long lunch together.

Sir George had recently completed his lengthy and exhausting service as chairman of the Parades Commission, which regulates sectarian parades in Northern Ireland. This is a thankless and complicated task, calling for balance, wisdom, and courage. He seemed relaxed and looking forward to his renewed retirement. Six months later, at age eighty-three, he was dead of a massive heart attack while attending church. He will leave a vacuum in Northern Ireland that will not soon, if ever, be filled.

That evening, we returned to Deanes for dinner with Father Myles Kavanagh; Sister Mary was unfortunately in the United States preparing for a Flax Trust event. As usual, Myles was his charming and charismatic self. The Brookfield Mill has had to downsize due to the global financial crisis that has affected government spending and private contributions. But the work goes on, and Myles seemed indefatigable and ageless.

The next morning turned out to be the hundredth anniversary of Covenant Day, which marks the signing of Ulster Covenant, organized by Sir Edward Carson, in which hundreds of unionists pledged (some by signing in their own blood) to remain part of the United Kingdom, by force of arms if necessary. Celebrated by some thirty thousand unionists with a mass march and parade from City Hall to Stormont and back, Covenant Day meant the central city was largely paralyzed for most of the day. Nevertheless, we made it across town to the Falls and the Shankill to meet with Geraldine McAteer and then Jackie Redpath.

Geraldine met us in the Falls Cultural Centre and coffee shop. Over tea, we talked about old times and the constant struggle on the Upper Springfield to find jobs, dignity, and a future. We were joined by Jackie, who shared much the same sentiments for his Shankill. Together, they both worried about the next generation of community leaders needed to take up the work.

Leaving the Falls, Jackie took us to his "local" for a pint on the Shankill Road. It turned out to be the very pub attacked by the Shankill Butchers during the height of the Troubles. In a display of black Irish humor, some wag had posted a sign advising "No Shooting." After a chat and some *craic* with the locals, we moved on to the other parts of the Shankill.

We traveled via the "Peace Gate" that connects the two neighborhoods and is still locked at night. But adjacent to the gate is a new mural painted on the side of a large building. It celebrates peace and peacemakers around the world and in Northern Ireland. (Jackie himself has a small cameo part.) The mural is a visual representation and symbol of all that has transpired in Northern Ireland and, when the gate is locked at night, what still needs to be done.

The following morning I had coffee at the hotel with Sammy Douglas, now a DUP member of the Local Assembly. Energetic as ever, Sammy had turned the East Belfast Partnership over to his daughter, a lawyer with administrative skills and a keen eye for the needs of the neighborhood in which she was raised. EBP, like the Upper Springfield Trust and the Great Shankill Partnership, struggles for funding after the economic downturn of 2008. But like its sister organizations, the EBP carries on and remains committed to its purpose.

We left the next day and headed home. On the flight, I reviewed my notes of the trip and thought about how deeply Northern Ireland and its people, especially the community leaders and friends I had made, had touched my heart and soul. I renewed my resolve then to finish this book and make at least some feeble attempt at telling their stories and their heroic contributions. I hope to have done that, even though it has taken me some years to tell the story. At the very least, my time and experiences in Northern Ireland are part of my permanent being and were the quintessential experience of a lifetime. For that, I am forever humbled and grateful.

Acknowledgments

This book would not have been possible without the invaluable assistance of several groups and individuals.

First, my clients and colleagues at my law firm who supported me, indulged my absences, and allowed me to maintain dual public/private lives in Denver, Washington, Dublin, and Northern Ireland. This was before emails and texts, which meant long-distance faxes and early morning or late night phone calls, which they tolerated. My thanks and appreciation for their patience and understanding.

Second, my research assistant, Melissa Field. Her research and interviews in Northern Ireland, insights, and edits were invaluable. She is a remarkable young woman whose own story of courage and indomitable spirit merits telling and was an inspiration to me.

And, last but never least, my long-time secretary, executive assistant, chief of staff in time of war, and true friend, Donna Mather. In the more than thirty-six years we worked together, she brought skill, dedication, and judgment to her work and mine, both in the practice of law and in organizing and developing this book. She simply is the very best.

Made in the USA
Lexington, KY
17 October 2014